Ballymena
Edited by Heather Killingray

First published in Great Britain in 2004 by:
Young Writers
Remus House
Coltsfoot Drive
Peterborough
PE2 9JX
Telephone: 01733 890066
Website: www.youngwriters.co.uk

All Rights Reserved

© *Copyright Contributors 2004*

SB ISBN 1 84460 467 5

Foreword

Young Writers was established in 1991 and has been passionately devoted to the promotion of reading and writing in children and young adults ever since. The quest continues today. Young Writers remains as committed to engendering the fostering of burgeoning poetic and literary talent as ever.

This year's Young Writers competition has proven as vibrant and dynamic as ever and we are delighted to present a showcase of the best poetry from across the UK. Each poem has been carefully selected from a wealth of *Once Upon A Rhyme* entries before ultimately being published in this, our twelfth primary school poetry series.

Once again, we have been supremely impressed by the overall high quality of the entries we have received. The imagination, energy and creativity which has gone into each young writer's entry made choosing the best poems a challenging and often difficult but ultimately hugely rewarding task - the general high standard of the work submitted amply vindicating this opportunity to bring their poetry to a larger appreciative audience.

We sincerely hope you are pleased with our final selection and that you will enjoy *Once Upon A Rhyme Ballymena* for many years to come.

Contents

All Saints Primary School

Sarah Sweeney (9)	1
Orla Killough (9)	1
Adrienne Clerkin (8)	2
Kelly Reid (8)	2
Shannon Faith (9)	3
Conor O'Flaherty (10)	3
Levi Devlin (9)	4
Aine McKee (9)	4
Aileen Rocks (9)	5
Aidan Marrs (9)	5
Shannon Walsh (9)	6
Dylan McDonagh (9)	6
Mark Hegarty (9)	7
Niamh Donaghy (9)	7
Oisin Lindsay (9)	8
Katie Connolly (9)	8

Broughshane Primary School

Alan Hamilton (9)	9
Calvin Kernohan (9)	9
James Simpson (9)	10
Hannah McCooke (10)	10
Philip McCullough (8)	11
Christine Maybin (10)	11
Patrick Esler (9)	12
Katie Carrington (8)	12
Rachel Mairs (10)	13
Hayley Sloan (7)	13
Kathryn Hamilton (10)	14
Emily McCaughey (8)	14
Zara Douglas (8)	15
Claire Mackenzie (8)	15
Simon Cunningham (7)	16
Ryan Bradley (8)	16
Alan Adams (7)	16
Melissa Millar (11)	17
Leanne McCullough (10)	17
Andrew Millar (10)	18

Sophie McKee (9)	19
Warren Montgomery (10)	19
Catherine McCartney (9)	20
Darren McAlonan (10)	20
Jolon Cupples (10)	21
Gemma Mitchell (11)	21
David McGaughey (11)	22
Jordan McCrystal (11)	22
Ruth McMaster (10)	23
Keely McAleese (11)	23
Gary McKendry (10)	24
Matthew Biggerstaff (11)	24
David Murray (10)	25
Shannon Douglas (9)	26
Stuart McCarthy (10)	26
Alice McCaughey (9)	27
David Maybin (11)	27
Nicola Galbraith (9)	28
Michael Faith (10)	28
Jenni McCandless (10)	29
Adam McDowell (10)	29
Abigail Martin (10)	30
Kathryn O'Hara (10)	30
Stacey McGavock (10)	31
Jaymee O'Hara (7)	31
Chloe Kennedy (10)	32
Rachel Giles (9)	32
Caroline Richards (10)	33
Jack Thompson (10)	33
Bronagh Neeson (9)	34
Victoria Marcus (10)	34
Philip Cunningham (9)	35
Evie Carrington (9)	35
Hannah Wray (9)	36
Hollie Neeson (8)	37
Phebe Calderwood (8)	37
Natasha Greer (9)	38
Amy Sneddon (7)	38
Joseph Cross (8)	39
Jack Graham (7)	39
Jessica Boal (11)	40
Jonathan Kernohan (7)	40

Gemma Lindsay (11) 41
Rebekah McNabney (7) 41
Jason Adams (9) 42
Jason Nicoletti (8) 42
Eva Richards (8) 43
Amy Farquhar (9) 43
Nicole Connor (10) 44
Timothy Patton (11) 44
Joanne Stirling (8) 45
Nathan Reid (10) 45
Gemma McClean (9) 46
Amy Hunter (8) 46
Aoife Hunter (8) 47
Gayle Adams (9) 47
Chloe McGall (9) 48

Buick Memorial Primary School
Joel McElwee (10) 48
Rebecca Buick (9) 49
Suzanne Dickey (9) 49
Andrew Cooke (8) 50
Maisie Black (7) 50
Claire Hoy (9) 51
Reuben Lamont (8) 51
Stephanie Lennox (8) 52
Pauline Wilson (7) 52
Lynsey McQuillan (8) 52
Robbie Moore (7) 53
Leroy Millar (8) 53
Troy Ramsey (7) 53
Carly McIntosh (8) 54
Jayne Allen (9) 54
Kathryn McWhirter (9) 55
Jessica Reid (8) 55
Michael Reid (11) 56
Matthew McCallion (7) 56
Matthew Kennedy (10) 57
Sarah Houston (11) 57
Melissa McKay (8) 58
Jonathan Kerr (8) 58
Andrew Atcheson (8) 59

Daniel McElwee (8)	59
Daniel Knowles (11)	60
Jordan Henry (8)	60
Michael McKelvey (8)	61
Megan Rea (8)	61
Adam Henry (11)	62
Ross Little (10)	63
Stephen Kerr (10)	63
Matthew Adams (10)	64
Ben Coulter (11)	64
Daniel Bestek (7)	65
Charles Orr (7)	65
Amy Galbraith (7)	66
Michael Adams (8)	66
Ashley Marshall (11)	67
Curtis Murray (9)	67
Megan Robinson (11)	68
Pamela McBurney (9)	68
Mark McAuley (11)	69
Thomas Mellon (8)	69
Matthew Beattie (8)	70
Amy Watt (7)	70
Dannielle Shannon (8)	70
Ian Lamont (7)	71
Natalie Swann (7)	71
Andrew McClenaghan (8)	71
Matthew Morgan (8)	72
Gemma McClenaghan (8)	72
Judith Fenton (8)	72
Matthew Hanna (10)	73
Allison Rodgers (10)	73
Rachel Lowry (10)	73
Jonathan McCloy (9)	74
Alan Glenholmes (11)	74
Hannah Martin (10)	75
Peter Hayes (11)	75
Helen McKelvey (9)	76
Laura Beattie (10)	77
Amy Evans (10)	77
Adam Greer (7)	78
Mervyn Millar (9)	79
Jordan McCullough (9)	79

Luke Henry (8)	79
Jessica Todd (10)	80
Alannah Dickson (8)	80
April Morgan (9)	81
Claire Robinson (8)	81
Amy McCallion (10)	82
Leanne Holmes (9)	82
Ashleigh Campbell (11)	83
Darren Geddis (10)	83
Connor Booth (8)	83
Rachel Morrison (10)	84
Lauren Martin (9)	84
Jason Boal (7)	84
Rachel Currie (9)	85
Steven Kernohan (8)	85
Adam Buick (11)	86
Natasha Richmond (9)	86
Peter Irvine (11)	87
Ross Beattie (9)	87
Cherith Fenton (10)	88
Lyndsay Holmes (9)	88
Nicole McClintock (10)	89
Melissa Speers (10)	89
Scott Adams (8)	90
Naomi Finlay (8)	90
Thomas Gaston (8)	90

Carniny Primary School

Danielle McWhirter (7)	91
Craig Wright (7)	91
Holly Robinson (7)	92
Christopher Wills (7)	92
Ryan Douds (7)	93
Richard McCully (7)	93
Sarah Fullerton (7)	94
Neil McCluney (7)	94
Mark Ramsey (8)	95
Jenny Sutherland (8)	95
Sarah Kelso (8)	96
Kirsty McDowell (8)	96
Ben McCandless (8)	97

Megan Campbell (7)	97
Laura McCullough (8)	98
Christopher Dalrymple (11)	98
Zoë McLees (11)	99
Paul Johnston (8)	99
Zach Templeton (10)	100
Peter Rodgers (8)	100
Christie Law (10)	101
Ryan Dowds (7)	101
Christopher Quigley (10)	102
Christopher Cameron (11)	102
Mark Herbison (11)	103
Emma Rose (11)	103
Paul McCrory (10)	103
Connor Worthington (9)	104
Clinton McKeown (11)	104
Nichola Kennedy (11)	105
Gemma Jackson (12)	105
Samantha Lowry (11)	105
Matthew O'Neill (9)	106
Marc Law (10)	106
Lauren Davison (10)	106
Steven Carruthers (10)	107
Hannah Mckillop (9)	107
Jack Murray (9)	107
Leah Wright (10)	108
Simon Boyd (10)	108
Robbie Sutherland (9)	109
Nicolle Scroggie (10)	109
Kimberley Carmichael (9)	110
Lauren Neilly (9)	110
Lauren McNair (9)	111
Stephen Leetch (9)	111
Kelly McCloy (9)	112
Matthew Booth (10)	112
Gillian Hutchinson (9)	112
Joel Scullion (10)	113

Kells And Connor Primary School

Carl Sloan (10)	113
Gemma Scott (10)	114

Michael Davidson (9)	114
Jonathan Erwin (9)	115
Edwina Taylor (10)	115
Richard French (9)	116
Anthony Craig (10)	116
John Mawhinney (9)	117
Samantha Magill (10)	118
Mark Smyth (9)	119
Emma Hutchinson (9)	120
Rachel Martin (10)	120
Colin Price (9)	121
Rebecca Feeney (10)	121
Kim White (10)	122
Jonathan Caldwell (10)	122
Bethany Brown (9)	123
Samuel McIlveen (9)	123

Longstone Primary School

Gemma Dickey (11)	124
Tamara Marshall (9)	124
Jonathan Kerr (8)	125
Robynne Cameron (9)	125
Nathan Dickey (9)	125
Jack Johnston (9)	126
Samuel Finlay (9)	126

Moorfields Primary School

Daniel McKillen (10)	126
Stewart McIlwaine (10)	127
Christine Freckingham (10)	127
Emma Dawson (10)	128
Ruth Walker (11)	128
Kristoffer Steele (11)	129
David White (11)	129
Lucinda Ellis (10)	129
Donna McCord (11)	130
Gemma Russell (10)	130
Andrew Ellison (11)	131
Adam Brown (10)	131
Angus Gibson (11)	132
Laura Handley (10)	132

Jonathan Nevin (11) 133
Rebecca Warwick (10) 133
Caleb Morrison (11) 134
Aaron Cairns (10) 134

St Mary's Primary School, Cushendall
Darren McLaughlin (8) 135
Sean McAfee (10) 135
Cliodhna Maskey (8) 136
Hannah McAlister (8) 136
Sarah Morgan (8) 137
Dominic Delargy (10) 137
Soracha Cosgrove (9) 138
Katie Bowen (10) 138
Eoin McManus (8) 139
Eoghan Allen (9) 139
Paul McCurry (8) 140
Leanne McKeegan (10) 140
Fiona Rowan (9) 141
Clare Morgan (10) 141
Shaun O'Boyle (9) 142
Patrick Blaney (10) 142
Alex Delargy (8) 143
Sarah Callaghan (9) 143
Caoimhe McManus (10) 144
Kathryn McIlroy (9) 145
Leona McAuley (9) 146
Moira Molloy (10) 146
Declan McAlister (9) 147
Andrew Delargy (10) 147
Conor McAlister (10) 148
Stephen McAuley (9) 149
Maria Kane (9) 149

St Mary's Primary School, Greenlough
Caolan Diamond (7) 150
Michael Henry (8) 150
Ryan McGoldrick (8) 150
Erin O'Neill (8) 151
Paul Carey (8) 151
Niall Loughlin (8) 151

Aimee Cassidy (8)	152
Seanin Marron (8)	152
Emma Mooney (7)	152
Breandán McNally (8)	153
Catherine Morren (8)	153
Tomás Madden (8)	154
Aimée Bedell (8)	154
Laura McCallion (8)	154
Aidan McErlean (7)	155
Jonathan McAteer (8)	155
Brendan Laverty (7)	155
Gráinne Maguire (8)	156
Clare Doherty (9)	157
Emma McErlain (8)	157
Catherine Hegarty (9)	158
James Duffin (9)	158
Liam Quinn (9)	159
Piaras McGarry (8)	159
Roisin McCloskey (8)	160
Robert Kelly (9)	160
Colleen McErlean (9)	161
Christopher McPeake (8)	161
Olivia Hamill (9)	162
Geraldine Scullin (10)	162
Michael Kearney (10)	163
Declan Laverty (10)	163
Michael McCann (8)	163
Sarah-Louise McPeake (9)	164
Stephen Cassidy (10)	164
Michael McCloskey (10)	164
Connor McAllister (10)	165
Cathal McGurk (10)	165
Brid Mackle (10)	165
Michael Scullin (10)	166
Matthew Henry (9)	166
Enda McNally (10)	166
Fionnuala Scullin (9)	167

The Diamond Primary School

Joanne Rodgers (9)	167
Gareth Workman (10)	168

Beverley Kerr (11)	168
Nicola Simpson (10)	169
Matthew Kirk (7)	169
Reuben Bailie (8)	170
Amy Greer (11)	170
Lee Millar (9)	171
Trevor Holmes (8)	171
Hannah Kirk (8)	172
Kirsty Speers (7)	172
Jonathan Jordan (9)	173
Gareth Harkness (9)	173
Janelle McCloy (9)	174
Ryan Smyth (9)	175
Stewart McDonald (8)	175
David Simpson (8)	176
Mark Patterson (7)	176
Victoria Henry (9)	177
Hannah Smyth (7)	177

The Poems

Nursery Rhymes

The cat and the mouse
they started to shout because the cat
wanted to eat the mouse
the mouse wanted to eat the cat
the cat started to laugh
you silly old mouse
you couldn't get me
into your wee mouth
then started to shout once again
the mouse stopped shouting
so did the cat
then the mouse
said something he wished he never said
because the cat
started chasing him again
then left him for some other cat
to chase him.

Sarah Sweeney (9)
All Saints Primary School

Make-Believe

I have everything in the world
And you know what
I'll get myself
With my own money,

I don't get pocket money
Not even from my relations,
I ask if I could wash the dishes
Wash the car
No, no and no!
They say it every time.

But do you want to
Know how I get it
With my imagination.

Orla Killough (9)
All Saints Primary School

A Visit To Watertop Farm

When I saw the cuddly,
furry puppies at Watertop farm,
I wanted to keep them for my
sister and I,
I had a plan.

When it was my turn to ride the horse,
I was about to ask the girl
who was leading it,
if I could have a puppy,
but my five year old cousin Aaron
and my uncle Jon,
came along and ruined my plan.

So I had another plan,
on my birthday in June,
I would go to Watertop Farm,
with my mum and dad,
and go on the horse by myself,
and nobody could disturb me.

Adrienne Clerkin (8)
All Saints Primary School

On Holiday

When we went on holiday to Ibiza,
My little silly billy sister pushed me
into the pool.

We stayed in an apartment
not a hotel,
It was very high indeed,
We had two balconies,
One was bigger
than the other one.

Kelly Reid (8)
All Saints Primary School

Holiday

Holidays are really fun
because all the work is done.
Monday, Tuesday, Wednesday, Thursday, Friday.
No school today,
you can have a lie in or
even go out and play.
In the holidays you can
do whatever you like.
Go on your skipping rope
or go for a ride on your bike.
When it's tea time
go to Burger King, why not?
Then it's time to get your pyjamas on
Get them on and come down.
Stay up to 12 o'clock
tired and sleepily walk up the stairs
brush your teeth and get into bed
Mummy comes and tucks you in.
It takes you a little while to get to sleep
but you finally manage without a peep.

Shannon Faith (9)
All Saints Primary School

Holidays

I would love to go to Spain
but the journey is too long and I
would hate to get sick.
And most of all
I don't know the way.
Next time I go on holiday,
I'll just go to Paris
so I don't get as home sick.

Conor O'Flaherty (10)
All Saints Primary School

Holidays

Holidays are fun
When I go to the beach
I play with my friends
And I have so much fun.
When the time is up
And the sun is upsetting
I go home and I have no fun.

I lie in bed
I think of all the holidays I had
I went to the beach
I play with my friends
And that is all the things I did.

Levi Devlin (9)
All Saints Primary School

Diamond

I have a precious diamond,
She is big and fat
I keep her on my bookshelf
I would like her on my mat.
I play with her all day,
She never goes away,
She will never break,
We'd stay up really late,
I used to want her so much I'd wish,
For diamond is my pet goldfish.

Aine McKee (9)
All Saints Primary School

I Believe . . .

I don't believe the sun is yellow,
nor orange or red,
but I do believe it is blue,
turquoise or something like that.
I don't believe the world is round,
I think it is triangular,
pointy and bumpy,
(especially with all those mountains).

I don't believe that dogs are
soft and cute,

But what I do believe
what I do believe is

We're all special.

Aileen Rocks (9)
All Saints Primary School

Seasons

Spring is the season
and winter is when you have
snowball fights.
Autumn is when you
play in the leaves
and last of all summer.
Summer is when you
go to the beach
and go up the sandhills
and go body surfing
if the waves are big.
When you come out
you dry off
and have a picnic.

Aidan Marrs (9)
All Saints Primary School

I Believe In

I believe in,
fairy tales
palaces and enchanted places.
I believe in
things that don't even exist
things that scare me,
and even . . .
even . . .
things and stuff
and things that aren't even stuff
or anything
ask me to believe in something
anything and I will.

Shannon Walsh (9)
All Saints Primary School

Seasons

Spring is the season
when the lambs come out
you always see them running about.
Summer is the season
when the birds fly in the sky.
Autumn is the season
when leaves are falling
and you always hear the
crows calling.
Winter is the season
when I am freezing
and I have to wrap up well.

Dylan McDonagh (9)
All Saints Primary School

Seasons

The hottest season of all is summer.
When children play merrily every day.
Winter is the coldest season
because everybody is totally freezing,
you need to wear warm clothes.
Spring is when the baby lambs come out
running, dancing, prancing about,
and all the birds are chirping and singing,
look at us flying.
Autumn is when all the leaves fall,
and all the crows begin to call.

Mark Hegarty (9)
All Saints Primary School

In School

In school
I love to play
me and my friend.
I play at breaktime and lunchtime.
Whatever day
I like to play
but when it is time to go home
no play!
but I still have
fun the next day.

Niamh Donaghy (9)
All Saints Primary School

Seasons

Every day I see things in the season
Red, green or blue.
Something old,
Something new,
Whatever I do I see them.
One of the seasons
Spring, summer, autumn and winter
The four seasons of the year.
The flowers in the spring,
Sun of summer,
Autumn leaves fall from the trees.
In the winter the last season
In the trees a robin sings.

Oisin Lindsay (9)
All Saints Primary School

My Favourite Things

My favourite things
Are special, soft and cuddly
Don't forget they're stuffed
My favourite things are all around
That's right!
My favourite things are . . .
    Teddies.

Katie Connolly (9)
All Saints Primary School

The Fog!

Creeping through the misty town,
Silent as a ruined house,
Still rivers running all around
Waves crashing against the harbour wall,
Fog creeping up the street,
Trying to get everywhere.
Car lights blurring
Rain trickling on the ground,
Frost crunching under my feet.
Dark houses,
With roses ready to die in gardens.
Beaches quiet,
Nobody around,
Away in the distance
I see a ship,
But there is no noise around.
I start walking home,
Suddenly I stop.
I hear a noise
I don't know what.
But I think it is a shrill cry,
I wonder what is happening.

Alan Hamilton (9)
Broughshane Primary School

Snowflake

S nowballs firing from every direction,
N apkins folded ready for dinner.
O utside your hands go completely numb,
W oolly jumper which keeps you warm!
F ire blazing making you sleepy,
L iving in a lovely warm house.
A urora floating in the sky,
K indness floating in the air.
E ternal happiness in the snow.

Calvin Kernohan (9)
Broughshane Primary School

Young Writers - Once Upon A Rhyme Ballymena

The Fog!

A silent ship in the old grey water,
Grey like an old floor,
Grey like an old man's hair,
Grey like an old brick wall,
Grey like an old fence.

Silent like a stalking tiger,
Silent like a cloud in the air,
Like an old man on a bike,
Like an old abandoned house,
Like an old rusty bike.

Cold as an iceberg,
Cold as Antarctica,
Like a freezing day,
Like a bath full of snow,
Like a day of snow.

James Simpson (9)
Broughshane Primary School

Spring

Spring is my favourite time of year
So happy, lively, full of cheer.
Baby lambs and boxing hares,
Spring is the time to lose all cares
In the meadow by the lea
Doze in the shade of an apple tree
Dip your toes into the water
Soon the days will get much hotter
Listen to the cuckoo's song
This gentle breeze may soon be gone.

Hannah McCooke (10)
Broughshane Primary School

The Misty Day

Here comes the fog, like a man strolling in from
A hard day's work.
Like a ship drifting into port,
Like a swan gliding gracefully down the lake.

As grey as an old done donkey,
And drab like a concrete yard,
It's just like smoke, only it does not go away.

As silent as a bird flying through the air,
As quiet as a little mouse darting across the floor.
Like worms wriggling through the soil.

Like a chilly January morning,
As cold as a block of ice.
It makes me shiver when I look at the fog,
Without even going outside.

Philip McCullough (8)
Broughshane Primary School

Valentine's Day

Valentine's Day is all about love
And remember not to give your loved one a dove,
Please thank Cupid,
And don't be stupid,
Inside your heart is all heated,
Don't be silly and go and eat it,
The colour of Valentines is of course red,
So don't give her yellow or you'll end up dead,
Sing her a song or she might throw you out,
She'll kick and punch and give a big shout,
This is a poem for boys to read and remember,
And remember that Valentine's is not in December.

Christine Maybin (10)
Broughshane Primary School

The Fog

Silent as a squirrel's tail,
Dusty as an old floor,
Grey like a stone house,
Grey like stones at the seashore,
Grey like the sad girl's eyes,
Grey like an old man's hair,
Silent like the stalking tiger,
Like silent, dusty clouds,
Silent as sleep with dreams,
Silent as a block of ice,
Cold as a frosty night,
Like ice cubes,
Like a dead fish,
Like silent steel so cold,
Silent and cold like snow,
Like the ocean,
Like a cold statue in a park,
Grey like old cobwebs,
Like the wind in grass,
Like mizzling rain,
Like a bird gliding in the sky,
Like a swan on the water.

Patrick Esler (9)
Broughshane Primary School

Winter Is Coming

Icicles hanging from the window sills
Sparkling snowflakes come drifting down
Snowballs flying through the air
Landing on the thick, white ground.

Robins flying everywhere
Snow is lying on the path
Frosty days come and go
Cold, sparkling snow.

Katie Carrington (8)
Broughshane Primary School

Spring

Daffodils, new life
Baby animals, sunsets.

All the gorgeous sunsets,
In the bright red skies,
All the gorgeous sunsets,
As the robin flies.

All the pretty little flowers,
In the grass so green,
Each one holds their head up high,
They all want to be seen.

All the little animals,
In the fields all day,
They all follow their brothers and sisters,
In every single way.

All the chirpy little birds,
In the trees so tall,
The birds should know how to fly,
Or else they might just fall.

Rachel Mairs (10)
Broughshane Primary School

Snowflakes

Snowflakes fall swiftly and silently
To the ground they come and play
They twinkle and sparkle in the moonlight
They are cold and icy
I like to watch them come down and down.

I love to go and play with them
Snowflakes are amazing things
They are beautiful when they twinkle.

Hayley Sloan (7)
Broughshane Primary School

Spring

The yellow and golden daffodils,
The lambs' faint, soft cry,
The birds begin to make their nests
While the clouds drift across the sky.

The dew sparkles on the grass,
Rain showers short and sweet,
Worms wriggle across the ground,
They scurry around my feet.

The baby lambs and baby birds
Fill the days with laughter
Each one with their soft, sweet cry,
Together with their mothers to live happily ever after.

The orange and purple crocuses
The snowdrops in the lane
The buds flowering on the trees
New life has come again.

Kathryn Hamilton (10)
Broughshane Primary School

Winter

Winter is a lovely season
When I ask to go outside
I have a very good reason
Birds migrating, animals hibernating
Snow is falling hip-hip hooray
Let's go out and build a snowman
I wish it could last forever and ever
Oh yes! Winter is here -
Shortened days, longer nights,
Spring is just around the corner
Winter has nearly gone
But at least I have the memories
And they are very, very strong.

Emily McCaughey (8)
Broughshane Primary School

Winter Is Here!

Floating snowflakes fall
Silently to the ground
Snow is dancing all around
Puddles freezing over
Ponds are shining with ice
Winter is a lovely season.

Warm clothes we wear in winter
Slippery roads are here
Ice sparkles on the side road
Throw snowballs during winter
I love winter.

Zara Douglas (8)
Broughshane Primary School

Winter Is Here!

When on a winter morning
You wake up
Go to the window
And what do you see?
I see the snow
What can you see?

I get dressed
And go downstairs
And find a layer of snow
So let's build a snowman!

Claire Mackenzie (8)
Broughshane Primary School

Winter

Winter is a lovely time of the year
The snow falls softly
Icicles are hanging from window sills
It is very cold.

The roads are very slippy
Outside is covered with snow
Children love to laugh and play
But the snow just has to go!

Simon Cunningham (7)
Broughshane Primary School

Winter All Around Us

Everything started to freeze
Snow is so gentle
Icicles hang from trees
Frosty leafy trees - now bare.

Dancing snowflakes fall to the ground
Twirling snow in the air
We cry when we have to say goodbye
Winter is the best time of year!

Ryan Bradley (8)
Broughshane Primary School

Winter

Icicles hang on our window sills
On a frosty morning
Snowflakes are dancing at night
When the moonlight is out
Every night the puddles sparkle
What a beautiful time of year.

Alan Adams (7)
Broughshane Primary School

Be My Valentine

B lushing and looking away
E veryone laughs

M y eyes can't see
Y ou are so sweet

V iolets are so sweet just like you
A hug or smile and I am happy
L ove letters coming and going through my
   door all day long
E verlasting love is in the air
N ot forever - oh no
T eddies to cuddle all night long
'I love you' said one teddy to me just like you did
N ights and I dream of you
E veryone is happy at the end of it all

Melissa Millar (11)
Broughshane Primary School

Spring

Spring is an exciting time of year for me,
When all the leaves are growing on the trees.

I love spring when the sun comes up,
All the little lambs playing with the pups.

See all the fields where the flowers are growing,
And all the farmers are out mowing.

Summer is coming round the corner soon,
But now it's time for bed,
Out comes the moon.

Leanne McCullough (10)
Broughshane Primary School

My Pets

I have two fish,
Their names are Bubbles and Goldie
They are bright orange in colour,
With a little speckle of black.
They swim around and around,
'Til they make me dizzy.
That is the story of my pet fish.

I have two budgies,
Their names are Beni and Tweety.
One is blue and one is yellow,
Chirping here and chirping there.
Oh what a chirping noise they make,
That is the story of my pet budgies.

I have two rabbits,
Their names are Fluffy and Socks.
They both are brown in colour,
With a little piece of white.
They scurry around in their hutch,
That is the story of my pet rabbits.

I have two dogs,
Their names are Sandy and Lucy.
Lucy is a black and white Jack Russell,
And Sandy is a Golden Labrador.
They sometimes play,
They sometimes fight,
That is the story of my pet dogs.

Andrew Millar (10)
Broughshane Primary School

My Cat Tess

When I see a mess,
It always comes from Tess.
Yesterday she caught a mouse,
And brought it into the house.
We love playing tag,
Until she ruined my bag.
She sits on that chair,
While watching the mayor.
I feed Jess under the table,
But she doesn't like being fed by Mable.
Tess loves chicken in jelly,
Because it is good for her belly.
She is very furry,
And is allergic to curry.
Tess used to sit on my knees,
Until she caught fleas.
She belongs to the group of tortoise shells!
When she wants food she can yell!
Jess has a white tip on her tail,
And is a nice female.

I love my cat *Tess!*

Sophie McKee (9)
Broughshane Primary School

D'Arcy My Dog

D 'Arcy loves to play with her bone to chew it all day
A lways likes to eat her food and likes scraps
R eally in a very good mood happily running about
C razy but good hearted very loving, caring and happy
Y ou truly are the best puppy in the world.

Warren Montgomery (10)
Broughshane Primary School

My Pal

In the summer we play rough
We sometimes play Blind Man's Bluff.
When Mum turns on the light,
She gives us both a fright.

When we have a sleepover, she is all mine,
For all that time.
In the morning we do our hair,
Then we go to the fair.

We have so much fun
When we bake a cake or a bun
Today we are going to make
A lovely, delicious cake.

We may not be the best kids on the block,
But when we are together we really rock.

Catherine McCartney (9)
Broughshane Primary School

Summer

Summer is the time of year we have fun,
We play football, rugby and volleyball.
We swim in the pool and play in the park,
And wear sun lotion so we don't get burnt.

Go to the beach and play in the water,
Eat lollipops and go to theme parks,
Never inside always out
I love summer.

Darren McAlonan (10)
Broughshane Primary School

The Park

In the park the people play
They play football and rugby too
In the park where there are picnics
People play fetch with dogs and sticks.

In the park there are children
They feed the ducks in the pond.

In the park there is a shop,
You can buy ice lollies when you are too hot
In the park there is a lot of heat,
You burn your bum if you sit in a seat.

In the park there are shrubs, trees and not forgetting,
The water fountain too.

Jolon Cupples (10)
Broughshane Primary School

Valentines

V iolet flowers are popular on this day
A ll teddy bears are loved
L ove is in the air
E njoyable dinners are being eaten
N obody is unhappy
T oo many people are being hugged
I 'm going to disco
N ice sweet cards
E njoy the day
S ongs for people in love.

Gemma Mitchell (11)
Broughshane Primary School

Autumn

Trees lose their leaves,
Lots and lots of leaves.
Ash keys,
Falling from ash trees.
Crunch, crunch, go the leaves,
Below children's feet.
Children jumping in
Piles of leaves.
People eating hot food,
Wearing warm clothes.
Loving mums wrap up
Happy children,
The frost will soon be
Here.

David McGaughey (11)
Broughshane Primary School

City Life

T he shops are open
H otels are full
E verywhere is busy

C abs on the street
I n the city you never get bored
T ime goes by fast
Y ou just want to go home and sleep.

Jordan McCrystal (11)
Broughshane Primary School

Going To The Moon!

G oing into a big rocket
O n the TV hearing 5, 4, 3, 2, 1 *blast off!*
I nto space off we go,
N ot knowing what we are doing,
G oing places having fun.

T o the moon,
O ff the ship.

T here are aliens,
H ere on the moon
E arth looks like a star from here.

M oving back to Earth,
O n the moon I say 'goodbye' to my alien friends.
O n the ship being sad,
N ot glad.

Ruth McMaster (10)
Broughshane Primary School

My Guinea Pig

My guinea pig is very cute
Very fat as well.
But most of all very friendly,
So I don't need a better guinea pig
When it suits me well.
All my friends think she's really cute,
So she must take it after me.

Keely McAleese (11)
Broughshane Primary School

No Way Home

I'm in jail
Waiting bail
For that crime
I lost every dime.

Now that I'm out
I stride about,
I found a comb
And write a poem.

The fire and flames
I got the blame
I walked to the pyre
And shed a tear.

This doesn't seem
To be a dream
Why can't I wake
To eat my birthday cake.

I met a man
With a dark tan,
Who said to me,
'Would you like some tea?'

I lost a part
Of my heart
This is the end
Will it mend?

Gary McKendry (10)
Broughshane Primary School

Summer

Flowers popping up to meet the sun
birds chirp in the trees,
bees buzzing in the air, summer is here,
cool drinks for all of us
I like summer.

Matthew Biggerstaff (11)
Broughshane Primary School

Larry The Lamb

Larry is a lamb
Not any old lamb
He is my special friend
And no one else would do.

When I was so ill
Larry was there for me
He helped to make me better
As well as you can see.

Now that I am better
And back on my feet
When I call my Larry
I can nearly hear him bleat.

Larry has travelled so many places
On trains, planes and automobiles
The only thing he cannot do
Is talk to other animals.

No matter where I go
Larry is always in tow
I never forget my mate
As he makes me feel so great.

Now that he is worn
Threadbare and thin
One thing's for sure
He will never go to the bin
Because I love him.

David Murray (10)
Broughshane Primary School

My Naughty Brother

My brother's name is Kristian,
We call him Kris sometimes.
Although he's only six years old,
He's naughty all the time.

He's got fair hair,
And blue eyes,
And isn't very tall,
When people see him
They think he's not bad at all.

He hides my shoes and books on me
He loses all my things
He's noisy and he shouts alot,
And thinks that he can sing.

I don't know why he's naughty
It could be just a game,
And even though he comes in my room,
I love him all the same.

Shannon Douglas (9)
Broughshane Primary School

Autumn Leaves

A utumn is here once again,
U nder the trees we pick leaves.
T iny leaves blow everywhere
U p on the hill we play conkers.
M um is busy making pies
N ice smells from the kitchen.

Stuart McCarthy (10)
Broughshane Primary School

Waking Up To Waste

Waste is a horrible thing
Just think
Would you like to wake up to waste?
Can you see it? I can.

Let's not wake up to waste
We'll *reduce,* how?
Reduce on litter
When we go for a walk have a small bag in stock.

Let's not wake up to waste
We'll *recycle,* how?
We can recycle anything
We can go to the Ecos Centre to recycle.

Let's not wake up to waste
We'll *reuse,* how?
We can reuse our plastic bags
We will take them back to the supermarket.

Alice McCaughey (9)
Broughshane Primary School

My Cats

M y cats are called Jack and Jill,
Y ou can pet them and they might lick you.

C hristine's cat is Jill,
A nd my cat is Jack,
T heir birthday is on the 2nd of April,
S aturday I play with them most.

David Maybin (11)
Broughshane Primary School

Young Writers - Once Upon A Rhyme Ballymena

Elf Magic

Elves dancing around the fairy tree
Leaving surprises for you and me
Enchanted forests, goblins and spells,
Pixies are playing tricks in the wells.

Fairies pulling faces in the sun
And the magic mushrooms are having fun,
Digging up long lost treasure
Having loads of fun and pleasure.

They have loads of portals here and there
One of them is to bumblebee bear
All sing a joyful song
Then up comes a rainbow so peaceful and long.

Nicola Galbraith (9)
Broughshane Primary School

Holly And Max

H olly and Max love to fight
O ff to play in the garden
L ove each other they do
L ying around the fire
Y ou're a very good dog Holly

   And

M ax and Holly are playing
A t the back of the shed
X is when my dogs play in the snow

Michael Faith (10)
Broughshane Primary School

Summer And Me

Why is summer nice for me?
Summer is nice for me because everywhere I look
Its colours I see.
Why is summer so happy and jolly?
It's happy and jolly because you don't need your brolly.

Why is it so much fun?
It's so much fun because you can go and play in the lovely big sun.
Why are there so many flowers?
There's so many because people sat planting them hour after hour.

Why is it almost completely sunny and bright?
It's almost, always sunny and bright because the sun stays up
Close to night.
So now you should know or close enough that, summer is

My favourite season.

Jenni McCandless (10)
Broughshane Primary School

My Pet Chloe

I have a wonderful pet called Chloe the cat,
She's never far from the heat on her favourite mat.
When she's full of fun she plays with her ball,
When it's a sunny day she lies on the wall.

After playing she lies on her rug
In the silver moonlight she chases a bug
She goes to cat shows
And wins prizes including bows.

When she's happy you can hear her purr
She brings a smile to my face when I look at her
And when summer comes she climbs up trees
And when she's running about she chases bees.

Adam McDowell (10)
Broughshane Primary School

The World's Greatest Dog

My dog is so wonderful
She really is my chum,
Whenever we get on with each other
She really is quite fun.

She has beautiful bright eyes
And a big wet nose
Sometimes she is . . .
A real big pose.

My dog's favourite food is chicken and sausage
Sometimes she is a bit like an ostrich
Her favourite treat is a bone
She is sometimes really a bit of a moan.

Her favourite thing is a walk
Whilst I talk and talk
She gets all dirty and wet
That's because she is a real cool pet.

Now I am finishing off the poem
I bet she is sleeping at home
Now this is the very end
She really is my best friend.

Abigail Martin (10)
Broughshane Primary School

Winter

It was a piercing night,
The blackness towered over the trees,
Like a big, black, bear.
In winter's home
The torches are ablaze
Lighting up the many towers
A home for the sleeping folk of the woodland.

Kathryn O'Hara (10)
Broughshane Primary School

The Rabbit Has A Habit

This rabbit has a habit
Of eating sardines and pickles.
Even though he's extremely old
He often gets the tickles.

This rabbit has a habit
Of dancing around in circles
He is a happy, jolly guy
But believes he can do miracles.

This rabbit has a habit
Of hopping around in his hutch,
He loves to eat sweet things,
But greens? . . . Not that much.

This rabbit has a habit
Of thinking he is cool
But when he tries to impress
Oh . . . it makes me drool.

This rabbit has a habit
Of being a loveable lad
He is so cute and fluffy
Somehow he makes me sad.

Stacey McGavock (10)
Broughshane Primary School

Winter

Winter is coming
Knocking on my door
It is a great season
And is here for a good reason.

The robin is about
Looking for food
A little redbreast
As red as fire.

Jaymee O'Hara (7)
Broughshane Primary School

Autumn

Leaves lying on the ground,
Like crunchy carrots,
Conkers hanging on the trees,
Like porcupines hanging upside down,
Leaves fall off the trees,
Like crayons falling off the rainbow.

My birthday is in autumn,
It seems very special to me,
Watching all the colours
Falling off the rainbow,
And having chips for tea,
Then playing with my presents,
Until it's time for bed.

Chloe Kennedy (10)
Broughshane Primary School

Jack Frost

I woke up this morning
and who did I see,
Jack Frost had come,
to be with me.

Now I'm happy so happy to say,
I shouted, 'Mum
I'm going out to play.'

Such fun I had,
Jack Frost and me,
Had such fun all day,
'Mum,' I shouted, 'I'm coming in to stay.'

Rachel Giles (9)
Broughshane Primary School

Christmas Day!

Turkey was first;
A great big balloon with legs.
Next was Brussels sprouts;
Disgusting time-bombs swathed in gravy.

Church now:
It was quite interesting today.
About how
Jesus changed the world.

Now presents!
Heavenly gifts from above.
Including
A pair of socks from my auntie Jo.
(How exciting).

I looked out,
And a woolly blanket of snow covered everything.
I went out,
And threw snowballs at Tibby, our cat.

It made me think,
About family values and stuff.
And whether Jesus
Had an Auntie Jo who gave Him socks.

Caroline Richards (10)
Broughshane Primary School

Christmas

The snow is like cotton wool balls
Santa sliding down a big dark cave
The presents are the colours of all the delicious fruits
The turkey is like a big brown balloon
Christmas reminds me of when Jesus was born.

Jack Thompson (10)
Broughshane Primary School

Birthdays!

When I woke up
I saw lots of presents,
Glowing in my room.

Is that cake?
It looks like a roundabout,
With nice creamy icing
It sort of reminds me of some,
Cotton wool.

Oh my goodness,
Is that a wrinkle?
Next thing you know
I'll be as old as a turtle.

Hey! but age doesn't matter
When you're having *fun!*

Bronagh Neeson (9)
Broughshane Primary School

Jack Frost

J ack Frost went out to play
A nd all the children ran away
C ome inside their mothers said
K eep nice and warm in your bed

F ireplaces were burning bright
R osy faces by the firelight
O ver the road Jack Frost sat
S ad that the children had stolen his hat
T omorrow morning I will be back for my hat before dawn.

Victoria Marcus (10)
Broughshane Primary School

Mrs Crossbox

Mrs Crossbox has grey strangly hair,
And wrinkled skin, but she couldn't care.
She lives in a school, in an old dusty store,
Some little mice live under the floor.

She uses old coats to make a bed,
For a pillow a chair, went under her head.
She was getting old and losing her sight,
And in the school there wasn't much light.

Her husband had died and her dog passed away,
She was really sad that very day.
Ever since she's felt alone,
She never talked to anyone on the phone.

Her best friends were the mice,
She thought they were very nice.
For her lunch, she had a school dinner,
But every day she was getting thinner.

Philip Cunningham (9)
Broughshane Primary School

Valentine's Day

Love is a gift sent from the heart.
It makes you feel warm, like a fire,
Inside every part.

Red shiny paper,
With presents inside,
Make your face shine,
With joy and pride.

Boys take girls out,
Kiss them goodnight,
And the doves hoot,
Until it is bright.

Evie Carrington (9)
Broughshane Primary School

The Fog!

Creeping through the misty town
Silent like a great white swan,
Gliding through the water.
Watching the land with sad grey eyes.
His cold grey eyes, hands touching the world around him.
Cold like your breath on an icy day,
Swirling mist, with a choking breath.
Creeping in the shadows.
Grey as an old dusty floor,
Like dust falling from an old chandelier.
Cold and dark,
Chilly and silent.
A silent ship gliding through the waters.
An angry face,
Filled with coldness,
No kindness,
In his heart at all.
Glowing fires in every house.
But on the doorstep,
Is where the fog stands.
Cold and dark,
Chilly and silent,
Swirling and still.
Always waiting to give someone a chill.

Hannah Wray (9)
Broughshane Primary School

The Fog

As still as a statue,
As still as a chair.
A silent ship gliding through the waves,
Making no sound passing by.
Silent as a glass lake.
Silent and cold as crystal snow,
Chilly as mist passing by,
My fingertips as cold as ice.
Fog is grey like a squirrel's bushy tail,
As silent as a tiger looking for its prey,
As cold as ice cubes floating in a jar,
As cold as watching fireworks
Exploding in the night sky.
As cold as a foggy morning,
As cold as the stars in the midnight sky.

Hollie Neeson (8)
Broughshane Primary School

Winter Is Coming

Icicles are hanging from the house
Puddles are frozen as hard as glass
Frosty mornings are coming too
Snow is falling making blankets
Birds flying in the beautiful snow
Let's go out and build a snowman.

Children love playing in the snow
Children enjoy making snow angels
Children love throwing snowballs
Children like making snowmen.

Phebe Calderwood (8)
Broughshane Primary School

The Fog

Fog is grey like a lovely squirrel's tail.
It is like a sad dog's poor eyes.
Grey like stones on a seashore.
It is cold as ice cubes, like crystal,
As the mist is passing by.
My fingertips are cold as ice,
Like frosty and cold nights.
Silent ships gliding through the waves,
Fog means death to all divers.
As still as a statue.
Silent like a stalking tiger after its prey.
Silent as a shelf of old books,
Like mizzling rain.

Natasha Greer (9)
Broughshane Primary School

Winter

It's winter, oh so cold!
My hands are like
Blocks of ice.
My toes are numb
My teeth chatter
Shivering all over
Winter is here.

Amy Sneddon (7)
Broughshane Primary School

Winter

Patterned snowflakes falling
All around us
Floating snow as well
As white as my kitten Snowbell.

I built a snowman
One sparkling morning
On its nose
Sat a robin
Its chest as red
As a cherry.

Joseph Cross (8)
Broughshane Primary School

Winter

Winter comes slippery roads
Icicles fall and slide
Frozen ponds all around
Children playing in the snow
Building snowmen.

Snow is great
Having snowball fights
Soon it's time for tea
A warm mug of cocoa
For me!

Jack Graham (7)
Broughshane Primary School

Horse Riding

H appy times I spend with horses,
O n a horse I spend most of my time,
R iding is what I enjoy,
S oaring over a jump is when I feel most happy,
E njoying their food, I brush their manes.

R iding up into the hills, is when I feel most
   relaxed,
I 'm on top of the world when I'm flying over a jump,
D ancing horses on the grass they go,
I 'm enjoying myself when I'm running a brush
   through a horse's tail,
N eighing as they canter down the fields,
G alloping is what I enjoy, the wind is in my
   hair, and it's just me and Pippin.

Jessica Boal (11)
Broughshane Primary School

Winter

Winter is a lovely time of year
Puddles turn to ice
Snowmen are getting built
The slippery roads are here.

Snowflakes fall softly
Freezing hands everywhere
Not a sound snowflakes make
Children playing with snowballs today.

Jonathan Kernohan (7)
Broughshane Primary School

The Big Tree

I'm lonely when it's windy
I'm lonely when I'm sad
I'm lonely when the leaves fall off and
leave me.

Happy in the morning when the sun is out
and bright
I'm happy then because everywhere is light.

At night I sway in the wind
my branches cry out to the flowers far below me.

I've got big arms that stretch out long and wide
I hug the other trees but they
sighed and cried.

I have been here so long the wood knows me well.

Gemma Lindsay (11)
Broughshane Primary School

Winter

W inter is here to stay!
 I cicles falling from window sills
N o nests seen in trees
T oday snow comes
E ven my dog is surprised
R iding around in the snow.

Rebekah McNabney (7)
Broughshane Primary School

Snowflakes

S ilvery frozen spiderwebs glowing over the silky white snow.
N ight skies covering the silent flaky snow.
O lives lying on the table beside the glowing night-fire.
W orthy woolly clothes worn in the afternoon snowfall.
F rozen flickery icicles falling and forming on the roof.
L ively light fires drying your gloves and socks.
A urora Borealis shading over the night sky.
K itchen warmth spoiling the cold crisp weather.
E nchanting snowflakes falling onto the windowsill.
S eason spirits falling on my nose.

Jason Adams (9)
Broughshane Primary School

Winter Is Here

Winter is here
Icicles hanging from the roofs
Snowflakes come to dance and play.

The snow is here
We have great fun
Walking through thick snow
Shiny icicles sparkle
The icy water is a puddle of glass.

Jason Nicoletti (8)
Broughshane Primary School

Springtime

The daffodils grow,
The bees fly around
Up and over,
Never touching the ground.

Poppies red, hyacinths blue,
Smelling very sweet
Waiting very happily
As roots spread round their feet.

All the old leaves disappear
Letting new ones grow
Colours, colours everywhere
As little buds start to show.

Eva Richards (8)
Broughshane Primary School

My Granny

My granny is so good to me,
She buys me lots of things
We make a great pair
We always go to the shops
And buy lots of things.

My granny is so kind
And loving to all of my cousins
We all love her so much
She's the best I will love her forever.

Amy Farquhar (9)
Broughshane Primary School

My Warrior Test

I am the ancient warrior of all times,
When Fionn MacCumhail is around,
Nobody whines!
When you have to run through the wood,
And jump trees as high as you could!
      Life wasn't easy!

Old monk he taught me the verses,
All I needed was useful nurses!
I was in pain,
I must admit I wasn't brave,
So don't be afraid!
As I say life wasn't easy!

Motto
'Purity in our hearts,
Strength in our arms,
Truth in our lips.'

And the hardest part was
Writing this.

As I said life wasn't easy . . .

Nicole Connor (10)
Broughshane Primary School

Summer

S un is shining so bright,
U mbrellas up on the beach,
M ummies who buy ice cream,
M ornings are brighter,
E veryone out in the sun,
R eady to play.

Timothy Patton (11)
Broughshane Primary School

Young Writers - Once Upon A Rhyme Ballymena

Granny

My granny loves me
She always makes me tea
She's the best granny
That I will ever see.

She's getting very old
That's what I was told
I'll have to buy her something
Maybe a pot of gold.

She buys me lots of things
Just like shiny gold rings
I love her so much
And I'm sure she loves me.

Joanne Stirling (8)
Broughshane Primary School

Saturday Morning

Football, a crazy game.
Take a penalty or free kick
and feel good.
We hear the whistle and
take a break.
I pass the ball.
It flies down the pitch
my heart soars
I scored a goal.

Nathan Reid (10)
Broughshane Primary School

My Little Sister!

My little sister is only two
Her nickname is Lucy Lu
She thinks she is the boss of me
But she is the best sister ever!

When we take her to the pool
She always acts a fool
And she tries to drink the water
She is so cute in her bikini!

Lucy Lu kicks me out of my room
And then she looks so gloom
See Lucy and I, share a room together
But we will love each other forever!

Gemma McClean (9)
Broughshane Primary School

Valentines

V alentine's Day is full of love
A heart can never be broken
L ove is always everywhere
E ven dogs, cats, are in love
N obody's ever scared to send a card
T o the ones they love
I sn't it very nice that we have Valentine's Day
N ever a sad day in Valentines
E ven children are having fun
S piders are in the cupboards.

Amy Hunter (8)
Broughshane Primary School

My Dog

My dog is so lively,
She runs about the house,
Playing games,
Knocking the lamp down,
She really is in a hurry.

We took my dog for a walk one day,
Eating grass and that,
I think that's normal,
It's getting near bedtime,
I say . . .
Go to bed Meg,
It's time for bed.

Aoife Hunter (8)
Broughshane Primary School

Valentine's Day

Valentine's Day is a day of love
And that love can't be broken
With all the flowers and all the chocolates
All the girls are happy that day
A fancy meal, a fancy present
Valentine's Day is a happy day.

Gayle Adams (9)
Broughshane Primary School

My School

I go to Broughshane Primary School
The teachers are so bossy
They make you work all day long
Maths and English all the time
It's about time the bell rang!

My favourite subject is History
We find out lots of mysteries
My least favourite subject is Maths
I hate dividing and subtracting.

Chloe McGall (9)
Broughshane Primary School

Minibeasts

W earing black and yellow stripes
A lmost impossible to predict
S imple creatures
P hysically flying minibeast
S treamlined!

A n insect
N ature created them
D angerous

B umblebees
E at honey
E nergetically!

Joel McElwee (10)
Buick Memorial Primary School

Then

A peaceful, clear stream
Tiny, beautiful flowers
A tall, strong apple tree
Robins chirping their sweet song
Running clear stream
Cows mooing peacefully
Happy, in the touch of fresh green grass.

Now

Horrible saws have cut down the beautiful apple tree.
Lots of ugly rubbish litter all
The clear stream soiled by chemicals and oil
Noisy cars racing endlessly by
A gunshot wounds a beautiful crow
Cows roar in pain as jagged glass rips their mouths.

I feel angry at what man has done.

Rebecca Buick (9)
Buick Memorial Primary School

Summer

We're off for a holiday,
No school just play!

We went off to the park
And stayed there until dark.

We went on the boat
And I started to gloat.

I was swimming in the sea
When I got stung with a bee.

We had an ice cream
Sitting by the stream.

Suzanne Dickey (9)
Buick Memorial Primary School

A Beautiful Field

2000
A tall, majestic tree
The softest grass you can ever feel
Lovely sparkling, cold stream
Bluetits singing peacefully in their nests
Wind breezing gently in the air
Streams splashing loudly over the stones.

Relaxed, in the feeling of the soft grass in my hand
Excited in the countryside.

2004
Now the tree has been knocked down to the ground
Litter lying on the soft grass
And animals dying from polluted water
The beautiful bluetits tangled in plastic pain
The soft grass is hard now and is polluted
The crash of a bottle chucked against a stone.

Deep anger because this place is ruined
Nature destroyed forever.

Andrew Cooke (8)
Buick Memorial Primary School

A Sense Of War

I see people dying,
I see bombs falling,
I smell the disgusting blood of dying.
I taste the salty tears on my lips.
I hear bombs falling.
I touch a loving hand.

Maisie Black (7)
Buick Memorial Primary School

Now And Then

1999
I saw:
A crystal-flowing river,
Beautiful brown and red leaves,
White and yellow daisies, so still and peaceful.
I heard:
The crunch of the fallen leaves under my feet
A robin so sweetly singing,
The flow of the tinkling river.
I felt:
Happy to touch the rough bark of the ancient
Beech tree.

2004
I see:
The dirt of the flowing stream, so dangerous to all
the wild life.
All the beautiful leaves and trees are gone
Instead there are ugly, sprawling houses.
I hear:
The roar of speeding cars, not so peaceful now.
Impatient beeping of a horn so horrible
The smash of tossed-away breaking glass
I feel:
So very sorry that this has happened to all the
creatures here.

Claire Hoy (9)
Buick Memorial Primary School

A Sense Of War

I see blood of the dead people
I smell bombing houses on fire
I hear shooting guns!
I taste smokescreens
I touch the loving hand of God.

Reuben Lamont (8)
Buick Memorial Primary School

The Week

As sad as Monday
As nice as Tuesday
As good as Wednesday
As musical as Thursday
As happy as Friday
As busy as Saturday
As energetic as Sunday.

Stephanie Lennox (8)
Buick Memorial Primary School

The Week

As moany as Monday
As boring as Tuesday
As energetic as Wednesday
As musical as Thursday
As lucky as Friday
As busy as Saturday
As sleepy as Sunday.

Pauline Wilson (7)
Buick Memorial Primary School

The Week

As sad as Monday
As horsy as Tuesday
As energetic as Wednesday
As musical as Thursday
As fun as Friday
As jumpy as Saturday
As restful as Sunday.

Lynsey McQuillan (8)
Buick Memorial Primary School

The Week

As sad as Monday
As fun as Tuesday
As halfway as Wednesday
As musical as Thursday
As fun as Friday
As happy as Saturday
As lazy as Sunday.

Robbie Moore (7)
Buick Memorial Primary School

A Sense Of War

I see the bombs exploding all around us
I hear the guns shooting every day and the
Soldiers marching
I smell the blood of the injured
I taste war on my food
I reach and touch the beautiful flowers.

Leroy Millar (8)
Buick Memorial Primary School

A Sense Of War

I see the homes on fire
I smell the blood of dying people
I taste the smell of exploding bombs
I hear the gun shooting
I touch my best friend for the last time.

Troy Ramsey (7)
Buick Memorial Primary School

A Sense Of War

I see the exploding bombs
Falling from the sky.

I see all the frightened people
Running away.

I smell the people and their fear.

I smell all the soldiers waiting to kill.

I taste the salty tears on my lips.

I taste the red blood too.

I hear all the people screaming and shouting.

I touch my family for a kiss goodbye.

Carly McIntosh (8)
Buick Memorial Primary School

Death Of A Field

A tall spreading oak tree
Pretty flowers, flowing stream
Lovely robins singing
Rustling leaves, rippling water over stones,
Happy in the field of the soft rabbit . . .

Stumps stick up where lovely trees have been cut down
Piles of rotten, ugly, disgusting rubbish
Houses built in huddles in the big beautiful field
Rob the birds of their hedgerow houses.

I feel angers by this disaster
Ashamed of this disgrace.

Jayne Allen (9)
Buick Memorial Primary School

The Change In Life

Peaceful fox and her cubs
Flowing sunlit stream
Colourful bird sitting on her nest
Greenfinches singing songs
Beautiful waterfall running
Bark crunching softly
Relaxed in the forest with the touch of the fox's
Warm fur.

The crunch of glass going into animals' feet
The oil spilt in the pond dirty and smelly
Piles of litter ugly and everywhere
The roar of diggers
The glass bottles lie smashed on the ground
The noise of puffing huffing factories.

I feel angry that man has destroyed everything.

Kathryn McWhirter (9)
Buick Memorial Primary School

A Sense Of War

I see bombs falling from the sky.
I smell the fear of kids losing their parents.
I taste salty tears in my mouth.
I hear the bombs in my sleep.
Nothing left but the touch of a loving hand.

Jessica Reid (8)
Buick Memorial Primary School

Youth And Old Age

Old age and youth cannot live together
Youth is full of fun
Age is very scared
Youth likes football
Age likes to knit
Youth is full of excitement
Age is dull and grey
Youth is a bright day
Age is very old
Youth is power and strength
Age is weak and wrinkly
Youth is lots of fun
Age is boring
Age I don't like
Youth I do like.

Michael Reid (11)
Buick Memorial Primary School

A Sense Of War

I see the world through a gas mask
I smell the red blood
I hear shouting from people dying
I taste the fear
I touch my mother's soft hands.

Matthew McCallion (7)
Buick Memorial Primary School

Witches' Spell

Double, double, toil and trouble,
Fire burn and cauldron bubble.

Into my pot I will put
Eyes of a lizard and toe of a newt.

Next for this spell snake's venom,
Of rats' heads I'll need seven.

Heart of cow, and frog's rear legs,
Let us put in some cream eggs.

Come my children stir the pot,
Let's give Macbeth his worst thought.

Double, double, toil and trouble,
Fire burn and cauldron bubble.

Matthew Kennedy (10)
Buick Memorial Primary School

Witches' Spell

Double, double, toil and trouble,
Fire burn and cauldron bubble
Into it will go some eyes
Don't forget the rotten pies.
Next will come the horses' manes
Dropping in a few blocked veins.
Now it's time to add the eggs
And the dead rat's mouldy legs.
At the end we'll give it a whisk,
Macbeth's life will now be at risk!
Double, double, toil and trouble,
Fire burn and cauldron bubble.

Sarah Houston (11)
Buick Memorial Primary School

My Little Puppy

I have a cute pet
He is a puppy
(Guess what else I have)
I've got a guppy.

Puppy would love to eat till he's fat as a barrel
During both day and night
He wouldn't even care about
Whether it's dark or light.

In the morning I go downstairs
There's not a very nice sight
I look in the dog's cupboard
He's eaten all the dog food alright.

My dog should be asleep by now
It's the middle of the night
But he likes to look out the window
To stare at the moon's light.

This is what he likes to do
He likes to play with his toy
Jump and roll and run about
He's such a good boy!

Melissa McKay (8)
Buick Memorial Primary School

A Sense Of War

I see some miserable children
I see some horrified soldiers
I smell the gunpowder of the banging guns
I hears the screams of the wailing parents
I hear the booming from the aeroplanes above
I feel the salty tears running down my face
The everlasting loving touch of my parents.

Jonathan Kerr (8)
Buick Memorial Primary School

The Hoover

Snuff, snuff, snuff goes the hoover
Up and down the room
Whirr, whirr, whirr it goes busily
Suddenly it goes broom, broom.

Mummy says, 'What's wrong with it?'
I don't know anyway
But then it went back to normal
And I shouted, 'Hurray!'

Across and around the carpet
Sucking up all the dirt
Like us it sometimes has a break
But then gets back to work!

Andrew Atcheson (8)
Buick Memorial Primary School

Death Of Nature

Craft-looking fox, beautiful butterfly
Lovely, calm, shiny, clear stream trickling down tiny waterfalls
Birds singing their own songs and fresh breeze through grass.

Relaxed on this peaceful mountainside.

A busy road with lots of cars belching fumes
Litter thrown on those noisy verges
Cars taking the sounds of nature away

Shame that it has been changed by men.

Daniel McElwee (8)
Buick Memorial Primary School

Karting At Raceview

The excitement builds as I put on the gear:
The balaclava, the helmet, the racesuit,
Then down the stairs to the karts with their engines running;
The middle one's mine!
Sitting in the pits, the anticipation increasing,
Then the adrenalin rush as the barrier is raised.
Supreme concentration!
Flat out on the straight, foot to the floor;
Deep breath at a tricky corner,
Holding on to the throttle 'til the last second,
Praying I won't crash.
Sweaty palms, fighting with the steering,
Screaming engines, screeching tyres,
Exhaust fumes, burning rubber,
Every lap timed,
All too soon, it's over.
I feel the buzz as I leave.
Did I beat the lap record?
Not quite; maybe next time,
Can we come back tomorrow, Dad?

Daniel Knowles (11)
Buick Memorial Primary School

A Sense Of War

I see people dying and blood all around me.
I smell fear east and west.
I taste the salty tears on my lips.
I hear bombs exploding! Shooting guns and bricks falling!
Nothing left but the gentle hand of God.

Jordan Henry (8)
Buick Memorial Primary School

Always Believe In Dreams

Dreams can definitely come true
It happened to me once!
I had dreamt a dream
It was absolutely
Extraordinary!
I had gone back in time in a portal . . .
(To 1864 that was the year the telephone was invented)
I had gone to Alexander Graham Bell's house
It was filled with test tubes and things called
Telephone wires . . .

The next day I was having my breakfast
And my mum told me
About Alexander Graham Bell . . .

I felt quite strange at first!
Was this a dream or reality?

See, dreams can come true!

Michael McKelvey (8)
Buick Memorial Primary School

A Sense Of War

I see children being taken away
I smell the smoke from the blasting bombs
I hear the houses being bombed
I taste the salty tears running down my cheeks
Nothing left but to touch the loving hands of
My mummy and daddy
I feel so scared that I'll lose them.

Megan Rea (8)
Buick Memorial Primary School

The Cave, The Knight, The Dragon, The Battle

Up in the hills where no one goes,
In a cave a thundering moan lows,
The cave is a
Low stalagmiter, high stalagtiter,
Wet tunnel, deep cavern,
Who ever goes in, never comes out,
Until one day someone came out and about.

He was a knight with a gleaming mare,
He rode swiftly, swiftly through the air,
He was a,
Kingly knight, tremendous might,
Shining armour, shield and sword,
He strode before the cave,
He walked in, oh! he was brave!

He found the dragon, staring down,
The dragon saw him, as a clown,
The dragon was,
Red scaled, through the air it could've sailed,
Bloodthirsty, fire breather,
He used his pyro breath,
Bringing the knight to his death.

The knight dashed like a unicorn,
He leapt up high to the dragon's horn,
The battle was,
Long lasting, fire blasting,
Sword slashing, armour dashing,
The dragon threw him down, the deed was soon done,
The dragon blasted silver flame, soon the dragon won.

Adam Henry (11)
Buick Memorial Primary School

My Granny

My granny is cool
She's a supergran
She flies around with her knickers on over her tights
She saved the world twice from aliens
She even plays for a band called Groovy Grannies
She wrestled bears in South Dakota
She raced cheetahs in Katmandu
She got the Grim Reaper in an arm lock and
Took him down for the count
My granny is ageless and fearless
Of course my gran is full of imagination
But that is what makes my gran a cool dude!

Ross Little (10)
Buick Memorial Primary School

The Daisy

The daisy grows in a little clump,
Standing up on a little lump.

They look so beautiful bunching there,
And in the winter the spot's so bare.

They are so beautiful lining the lane,
And still when you make a daisy chain.

I really love their yellow and white,
And in the garden they look so bright.

Stephen Kerr (10)
Buick Memorial Primary School

Pizza

Pizza, pizza, lovely pizza
All different kinds
Deep pan, thin base
Stone baked, oven caked,
With cheese all over your face.

Pizza, pizza, lovely pizza
All different kinds
Pepperoni, Hawaiian,
Cheese sauce, tomato sauce,
With crumbs all over your vest.

Pizza, pizza, lovely pizza
All different kinds
Dough baked, sauce topped
Cheese and seeded crusts
With an order in for more.

Matthew Adams (10)
Buick Memorial Primary School

The Humbug

Stripped like a Zebra,
Hard to the tongue,
Suck it to death?
Or crunch it to a shell?
The buttermint taste
With the liquorice hint.
The oval bug shape
Like a sunflower seed,
Alert in their packets of row
A line of stripy delight tolls.
A long lasting confectionery
Making generations as happy as Larry!

A sweet thought.

Ben Coulter (11)
Buick Memorial Primary School

My Friend: The Funny Ball

The funny ball is my ball
It can even hit the wall!
At school it sits beside me
Even sometimes on my knee!
It helps when I do a test
It makes sure I am best.
The funny ball is like a pet
He doesn't like when he gets wet
He goes on lead like a dog
Even when he chases a frog!
My funny friend is a rugby ball
He likes it when he is kicked over the wall.

Daniel Bestek (7)
Buick Memorial Primary School

Caterpillar

C aterpillar: I'm a slimy sort of lad.
A pples are my favourite sort of food.
T errified when I see a human's foot!
E xcellent: the taste of juicy oak leaves.
R adish: a bad sort of food.
P rotect myself by slithering underground.
I mpish: I like playing tricks.
L eaf: a very nutritious thing.
L uxury: mmm the insects I meet!
A mphibians like frogs, my greatest enemy.
R ace: a horrible game because I always finish last.

Charles Orr (7)
Buick Memorial Primary School

Make-Believe

Now I know
There's no such thing
As a dinosaur
And other things!
But spaceships, animals,
Yes that's true
At least they're better than
Sticking your fingers with super glue!
Sometimes people say:
It's true that spiders are
The sweetest things . . .
To me they're fine
But I'm sure they can't write in rhyme!
All they can do is run up and down
Little mice can scuttle round the town.

Amy Galbraith (7)
Buick Memorial Primary School

Proud And Tall

The giraffes are eating the acacia leaves
On the treetops
Very proud and tall
Over the open grassland
Of North Africa.
The giraffes are wild.
In Africa the land is so flat.
Giraffes are very big.

Michael Adams (8)
Buick Memorial Primary School

Fruit Cocktail

Apples are amazing
Bananas are bouncy
Pineapples are popular
Melons are mighty
Coconuts are crazy
Apricots are awkward
Lemons are lazy
Kiwis are kind
Oranges are organised
Mangoes are moody
Grapefruits are great
Limes are lucky
Peaches are perfect
Pears are pests
Raspberries are rosy
Blackberries are boring
Blueberries are busy
Grapes are grateful
A cocktail of tastes.

Ashley Marshall (11)
Buick Memorial Primary School

Trees - Our Friends

Beautiful trees grew beside my garden wall
Even in rough storms they did not fall
Trees like them provide our wooden floors
They give us timber for tables and doors
Little creatures live under the bark
Safely protected in the dark
We play around the trees having fun
Or underneath we eat our picnic buns.

Curtis Murray (9)
Buick Memorial Primary School

Dogs

There are all different sizes of dogs.
Small dogs, big dogs, tall dogs, long dogs,
Fat dogs, and of course thin dogs.
And they all sleep, eat, lick, sit, slobber,
Drool, run, walk and love-to-lie-down dogs.

There are all different names of dogs.
Spot, Tobi, Tepi, Zeebow, Lucky, Bow,
Ben, Sparky, Todi and lots more.
And they all sleep, eat, lick, sit, slobber,
Drool, run, walk, and love-to-chase-ball dogs.

There are all different colours of dogs.
Black, brown, blonde, white, dappled,
Spotty and of course hairy dogs.
And they all sleep, eat, lick, sit, slobber,
Drool, run, walk and love-to-roll-over-dead dogs.

There are all different kinds of dogs.
German Shepherds, pointers, chowa-wa, Dalmatian,
Greyhound, Bloodhound, Great Dane, Scottish Terrier.
And they all sleep, eat, lick, sit, slobber,
Drool, run, walk and beg-for-attention dogs.

And I love them all!

Megan Robinson (11)
Buick Memorial Primary School

Licking Lucy (A Tongue Twister)

Lucky Licking Lucy licked her little lemon lolly.
A lovely licking lip-sticking lemon lolly it was.
So lucky Licking Lucy got a lot of lovely lemon lip-sticking lollies
to lick!

Pamela McBurney (9)
Buick Memorial Primary School

Joey Dunlop

Joey Dunlop you were the best
Your bright yellow crash helmet stood out from the rest.
You always were your own mechanic
So if anything went wrong you never were in a panic
You had 26TT wins
Your loyal fans raised a great din
There was no doubt about who was boss
You showed David Jefferys what you were made of
When you stuffed him in the formula one!
To find your equal there is none.

Mark McAuley (11)
Buick Memorial Primary School

My Favourite Animals

Animals are like air to me
Because they make me feel full of glee!
Puppies are like cuddly toys
But mostly I like puppies that are boys.
Rabbits are like spacehoppers
Their feet are like special flippers.
I like kittens they have lovely colours
I love them like they are my brothers.
Hamsters are like fluffy balls
You could find one in the hall.

Thomas Mellon (8)
Buick Memorial Primary School

The Crooked Man

There once was a crooked man
He had crooked teeth and crooked legs
He had a crooked tongue and crooked toes
He had crooked fingers and a crooked nose.

He went to a crooked street and to the market too,
He met his crooked friend and together
They went to the zoo!

Matthew Beattie (8)
Buick Memorial Primary School

Giants

G iants are humungous and strong
I rish giants are rich and have long hair
A nd some giants like to snore
N o giants are small
T oilets have to be big for giants!
S ome giants wear hats.

Amy Watt (7)
Buick Memorial Primary School

Teachers

Teachers are a menace!
They give us lots of work
They are cool and smart and funny
They are silly too when it is sunny!

Dannielle Shannon (8)
Buick Memorial Primary School

Giraffes: Beware!

The giraffe is standing
With its big long neck
When it's bending over
I hope it doesn't break!
When he's getting water
He'd better watch out
When he's doing the splits
His skin might rip!

Ian Lamont (7)
Buick Memorial Primary School

I Don't Like School!

I don't want to go to school
But have to, as it keeps Mum cool!
I'm on my way with coat, lunchbox and
Schoolbag,
I have to hurry
Oh what a drag!

Natalie Swann (7)
Buick Memorial Primary School

Who Are Giants?

G iants are big and round
 I think they could lift a shop
A nd they could eat lots of stuff
N obody can harm a giant
T he giant travels on his feet
S tamps on lots of people!

Andrew McClenaghan (8)
Buick Memorial Primary School

The Giraffe

The giraffe is big
Tall and strong
And he is proud of it
Nibbling away at the acacia leaves
Looking over the treetops
You can see them in North Africa on
The Savannah
They graze all day long
Yellow and black spots.

Matthew Morgan (8)
Buick Memorial Primary School

A Different Park

Playing in the park
On the slippery, silver slide
On the swings that look like rhino heads!
They *don't* scare me!
The see-saws look like crocodile tails
But in the park I feel free, free, free!

Gemma McClenaghan (8)
Buick Memorial Primary School

Fruit

Fruit is sometimes boring
Every time I am hungry
I wish I didn't have to eat anymore fruit!
I hate the look of fruit
But I have to eat it sometimes . . .
Or else my bones will not get healthy.

Judith Fenton (8)
Buick Memorial Primary School

Cat

The cat with those innocent eyes
Just before he pounces on that bird
He wiggles his bottom and bends down
Then how fast he runs! Wow!

He licks the milk up like it's the last
And eats that food up so fast!
He sleeps in that cosy bed
And doesn't even notice who goes by.

Matthew Hanna (10)
Buick Memorial Primary School

Tammy

Tammy is a beautiful English Collie
With a brown and white coat
Bright eyes and jolly
A loyal friend who's company
And very special, always to me.

Allison Rodgers (10)
Buick Memorial Primary School

Puzzle

I live in a burrow underground
I have ears that point up. I can be
A wild animal but I can also be
A pet. I love jumping.

Answer: Rabbit.

Rachel Lowry (10)
Buick Memorial Primary School

Young Writers - Once Upon A Rhyme Ballymena

Remote Controlled Quad

SSSSSSSSSSSSSSS
My quad is my favourite toy
It's fun for any boy!
It's a bit bigger than a loaf of bread
And it's coloured with red.
When you have the control
Use the wheels to make it roll
Press the button
It will start or stop
It's got springs under it
So you can even make it hop.
Forward. Back.
Racing round like a track
Left, right
For the dark it's got a light.
So much fun . . .
Till the battery goes done.
SSS SSS SSS ssss ss s s.

Jonathan McCloy (9)
Buick Memorial Primary School

Fruit

F ruit keeps you healthy.
R ound red apples.
U nique oranges, bananas and pears
I magine you were made of fruit
T ake it and eat yourself up.

Alan Glenholmes (11)
Buick Memorial Primary School

Inside My Head

In it there is a determination to get
Everything right.

There is excitement to play
And enjoy hockey and swimming.

There is the enjoyment to be around others.

The horror of going to a violin
Lesson without having practised.

There is a tree of attitudes and I pick one
Everyday.

There is a craving for sweet things once
In a while.

There is a fuss over how you look and
What you wear.

There is a sensitive spot that gets hurt
Every day.

There is an urge to comfort others when they're
Feeling sad.

There are mountains and valleys that represent my
Ups and downs.

Hannah Martin (10)
Buick Memorial Primary School

Anger!

Anger is dark red
It tastes like burnt tomatoes
And smells like gas.
It looks like fire mixed with gas
And sounds like a war field.
It feels like fire in your hand
Anger is red hot.

Peter Hayes (11)
Buick Memorial Primary School

Inside My Head - (A Girl's Head)

There is a different world
Bows and arrows
To drive away all thought of a flute lesson.

There is daydreaming
And drowsiness.

And there is a certain determination
To do my best and
Reach the top.

There is a jungle of magical creatures
And a forest of their names
And new ones are always forming.

There is long forgotten info
A times table or two
And where I made a secret sweet store.

There is a huge prison full
Of nasty thoughts about
What friends think of you.

Then there is a place,
A small room of
Love and kindness
That you cannot fail to find and call home.

There is excitement and life
Just waiting to be released
And to have some fun.

Helen McKelvey (9)
Buick Memorial Primary School

Inside My Head (A Girl's Head)

In it there is a school
Where we get lots of homework
For learning and going on trips.

And there is a park
To play in and
Have fun.

There are
Secrets, secrets
That might never
Be told.

There is a test
A test to get
Right.

There is sadness
There is happiness
There is excitement.

Laura Beattie (10)
Buick Memorial Primary School

Winter

Plop goes the rain against the window
Crash goes the lightning as a big fork appears.

I sit and hide my head under the covers
Hearing my parents saying the electricity has gone out.
My little brother begins to cry.

Flash, crash, plop, flash, crash, plop.
The winter has begun!

Amy Evans (10)
Buick Memorial Primary School

The Dream

Today was a bad day
The weather had got out of hand
It was rain all
Over the land.
Rain storms
Hurricanes
And floods
Ships and subs
And bath tubs.
Nearly floated and
Got dragged away
The sky, the Earth
The planet all grey.
People fled their
Homes taking
Their belongings
And their
Garden gnomes.
It seemed the
Rain would never stop
Then came the final drop.
The clouds disappeared
The sun came out
Hurrah they all began to shout!
I could hear a tap go plop, plop, plop
Just then I suddenly woke up!

Adam Greer (7)
Buick Memorial Primary School

Double Trouble At The Pool

There are people in the pool
And the lifeguard's looking cool
And a very fat swimmer
Wishes deeply she was thinner
A boy who only wants to waddle
And a toddler who can paddle
There are learners getting better
While the tiles are feeling wetter
Times up! The buzzer's hooting
To the changing-rooms they're scooting!

Mervyn Millar (9)
Buick Memorial Primary School

Apple Tree

I have an apple tree
It makes apples just for me
Under the bark
It is very dark
An apple falls on my head
And it is red.

Jordan McCullough (9)
Buick Memorial Primary School

The Giraffe

The giraffe is reaching up high
To the tree tops
Wandering among the acacia trees
Bending down to get a drink
With a very long neck
And a very strong neck
And a big long neck.

Luke Henry (8)
Buick Memorial Primary School

Inside My Head

Inside my head there is
Excitement and fun.

There is eagerness and
Nervousness.

There is a jungle of frills and fluffs,
Feathers and puffs
Representing my thoughts.

There is a river of laughter flowing all the
Time, (nearly).

There is a swimming pool of crunchy
Sweets which I visit a lot of the time.

There is a war of planes and bombs,
Guns and more to fight away the nasty thoughts.

There is a disaster when a hair springs
Out of your hairstyle.

There are puppies running
Around on a soft pillow, wanting their bellies scratched.

There is a mountain
I hike up to find my prize.

But best of all there is a room where I can love my family
And keep my secrets.

Jessica Todd (10)
Buick Memorial Primary School

The Snail

Snail moves very slowly on its foot.
Its home is a shell on its back.
Slowly, slowly the snail moves on.
Sticks close to fruit, grass, leaf and wall.
The snail slides and slithers
Down the garden path it slithers.
Do not touch its feelers or in they go.

Alannah Dickson (8)
Buick Memorial Primary School

The Red Back Spider

At night when the sun goes down,
Not a human to be found.
Out emerges the red back spider,
One of the arachnid's best-known hider.
Along comes a little black fly,
Flying quickly across the sky.
Does he not know what's dead ahead?
A sticky silken web.
With one silk string he is caught,
Although he should have stopped and thought,
But no he didn't, he did not.
Yum, yum said the spider who was a very good spider,
Who was a very good hider.
He sucked the blood while looking at the sky,
And that was the end of the fly!

April Morgan (9)
Buick Memorial Primary School

Autumn Senses

Autumn is dark and grey

Autumn tastes like nice warm tea and
roast potatoes with a lovely cup of soup.

It sounds like fireworks going up to
sparkle.

It looks like colourful leaves falling from
the trees.

It smells like fireworks, bonfires and smoke.

It makes me and my family feel free forever.

Claire Robinson (8)
Buick Memorial Primary School

Inside My Head

In it there is dancing
And going to sleep
And doing away with school.

There is
Going to W5
Which shall be in Easter.

And there is
A new cousin on the way
And a new cousin staying over,
And we can't wait.

There is a girl
Bouncing up and down.

There is homework.

There are no matters to worry about.

And I just can't wait.

Amy McCallion (10)
Buick Memorial Primary School

My Family

In my family there are three boys
Who never ever play with toys
'Cause they're too old
(Well, that's what I'm told!)

In my family are two twin girls
Who are as beautiful as silvery pearls
Their manners are very good
With visitors, or eating food.

In my family there is one Mum
Who makes boring things seem fun.
Every day Mummy makes me dinner
If she didn't we'd all be much thinner!

Leanne Holmes (9)
Buick Memorial Primary School

Dogs

Dogs are sometimes cute and fluffy
Maybe you'll end up with one that's scruffy
Slobber and dribble all over the place
They will always leave their trace
As everyone says, 'a dog is for life'.
Forever they will love you with all their might.
Their favourite word is woof! woof! woof!
Unlike a cat they are not aloof.
It wags its tail in pure delight
To come home to my fourteen dogs is quite a sight.

Ashleigh Campbell (11)
Buick Memorial Primary School

The Annoying Wasp

Last night there was a wasp at home
It flew about the whole house
It drove me totally mental
In fact I would rather have a mouse.

And when I tried to kill it
It stung me and flew away
But the next time I see that wasp
It will really have to pay.

Darren Geddis (10)
Buick Memorial Primary School

The Whale

W hales are mammals
H uge are the whales
A whale squirts water out of its back
L argest whales have teeth to hold their food
E ven whales can kill other whales
S adly whales are being hunted for oil.

Connor Booth (8)
Buick Memorial Primary School

Honeybee Acrostic

H oney is delicious I make it every day
O h! How I love nectar
N ourishing honey we all love to eat.
E veryone likes our scrumptious honey
Y es, I have made some tasty honey.
B uzzing about all day we eventually find some nectar to eat.
E veryone runs away when we come near because
                                          they might get stung
E veryone eats our honey.

Rachel Morrison (10)
Buick Memorial Primary School

In Autumn

In autumn the tree beside the school wall
Is covered with apples so shiny and small
The leaves come swirling - none till next year
Making the rustling sound I like to hear.

Lauren Martin (9)
Buick Memorial Primary School

Giants

Giants are big and tall
Giants are bad and naughty
Giants are selfish and lazy
Giants are greedy and scary.

Jason Boal (7)
Buick Memorial Primary School

And Time Goes On

Watch the horizon,
As the sun comes up
Springtime and life has begun,
Everything is fresh and new.

Midday - the sun peaks,
It is the height of summer,
Days are carefree and full of fun,
Short nights and long days ahead.

The sun is sinking,
Autumn leaves fall,
Feet move slowly along the path,
Crunch, crunch, crunch.

The evening has come quickly,
Dark days of winter are here.
We are older and wiser,
The sun goes down.

Rachel Currie (9)
Buick Memorial Primary School

Grape Acrostic

G reat grapes are lovely to eat
R ipe and yummy
A lways I eat them for break
P urple, red and green
E njoy them in a fruit salad.

Steven Kernohan (8)
Buick Memorial Primary School

Witches' Spell

Double, double, toil and trouble,
Fire burn and cauldron bubble.

Magic energy, now I command,
Come swiftly to me from all o'er the land.

Power deadly, power quick,
Like a poisonous snake's bite lick.

Powdered midnight, crumbled dawn,
The essence of owls' first song.

The fear in death, the hatred of life,
The terror in a young child's first strife.

When something small makes all undone,
When tiny moon blocks out big sun.

Vulpen cunning, feline wit,
Canine energy, time split.

The colour of darkness, the dullness of light
The pain and destruction of war, want and plight.

The movement of all things through time and space
Man will destroy all and leave no fresh place.

Double, double, toil and trouble,
Fire burn and cauldron bubble.

Adam Buick (11)
Buick Memorial Primary School

Apple Acrostic

A n apple is good and juicy.
P leasant to eat.
P lease eat one every day.
L ovely and healthy
E at them for your break.

Natasha Richmond (9)
Buick Memorial Primary School

My Macbeth Spell

Double, double, toil and trouble,
Fire burn and cauldron bubble.

Two rats heads in our giant pots,
One frog body without any spots.

One hundred flies I will need,
This will do my very bad deed.

Lungs from a robin, sound of a growl,
Two wings from a bat, two from an owl.

All part of our evil plot,
Will make Macbeth's heart stop!

Double, double, toil and trouble,
Fire burn and cauldron bubble.

Peter Irvine (11)
Buick Memorial Primary School

At The Fairground

'Fifty pence! Fifty pence!' calls the Candyfloss Man.
His voice can be heard over the bustling crowd.
The fairground is an exciting world.
I taste the sounds - like ice cream in different flavours.
I hear the bumper cars crashing and bashing.
I clamber into one,
And go leaping forwards.
Watch out!
Ouch! My neck!
I climb out and stroll over to the big wheel.
Up, up and up I sail,
I am a bird
Above a busy city.

Ross Beattie (9)
Buick Memorial Primary School

Witches' Spell

Double, double, toil and trouble
Fire burn and cauldron bubble.

Cats and bats and flattened rats
Just some more and that is that.

Pour in blood of the snake
That will taste just like some cake.

Have a little of the egg
More of cat and lizard's leg.

Now at the end we'll have the best
More of rat's blood and the rest.

Double, double, toil and trouble
Fire burn and cauldron bubble.

Cherith Fenton (10)
Buick Memorial Primary School

The Fair

I'm at the fair
I am having fun!
I've gone on all the rides,
My favourite one
Is the big wheel
I'm going on it again
Ahh!
I'm going round and round
Now I'm out
I feel sick!

Lyndsay Holmes (9)
Buick Memorial Primary School

Witches' Spell

Double, Double, toil and trouble
Fire burn and cauldron bubble

Into my cauldron I will put
Two frogs legs and an ogre's foot.

Then in my pot cow's eyes will go,
I hope this makes some trouble so.

Lungs of hens and hearts of fish,
This works with a thankful wish.

Come children stir the brew,
And get some homemade stew.

Double, double, toil and trouble,
Fire burn and cauldron bubble.

Nicole McClintock (10)
Buick Memorial Primary School

Witches' Spell

Double, double, toil and trouble
Fire burn and cauldron bubble.

Fur of a cat and wing of a bat,
Many long tails of filthy rats.

Two spider legs with a hare,
What a rolling delightful pair.

A rotting tongue of human man,
And two arms of man in a can.

Next in my hand a horse whip,
And two of people with a tip.

Double, double, toil and trouble
Fire burn and cauldron bubble.

Melissa Speers (10)
Buick Memorial Primary School

Weather Poem

Rain is falling like smashing glass,
Shattering in the mirrors below,
Stay inside or you'll get wet,
When it stops out you go!

You will smell the fresh air
And the dampness on the grass
Drips fall from the trees
On my shoulders as I pass.

Scott Adams (8)
Buick Memorial Primary School

My Dog

My dog is so cute
She plays with her toys
Running, rolling, squealing
I think she's laughing with me.
We're having so much fun
We leave our cares behind
And fall asleep at the end of the day.

Naomi Finlay (8)
Buick Memorial Primary School

Ben's Burger (Tongue-Twister)

Busy Ben bought a big burger from the butcher
Busy Ben brought the butcher's big burger back.
But Ben burnt the big burger black
Busy Ben buttered the big black burger he had brought back
Before he made a big black burger butty
With the big burger he had brought back from the butcher.

Thomas Gaston (8)
Buick Memorial Primary School

When I Was One

When I was one
I was very young.

When I was two
I went boo.

When I was three
I lost the key.

When I was four
I locked the door.

When I was five
I hit a hive.

When I was six
I did a trick.

When I was seven
I found a dog called Kevin.

Danielle McWhirter (7)
Carniny Primary School

School

S is for stickers on the wall
C is for Christopher in the hall
H is for Mr Henry, very tall
O is for oranges rolling round the hall
O is for outside with me and Ryan playing with the ball
L is for lights on the wall.

Craig Wright (7)
Carniny Primary School

In Come The Animals

In come the animals two by two
The ducks went quack and the cow went moo.
In come the animals three by three
There were two he's and also a she.
In come the animals four by four
The elephant was dancing at the door.
In come the animals five by five
But the kangaroo and the elephant weren't alive.
In come the animals six by six
The monkey is slapping the sticks.
In come the animals seven by seven
Some are bad, some are good and went to Heaven.
In comes the animals eight by eight
An elephant knocked down the gate.

Holly Robinson (7)
Carniny Primary School

In Come The Animals

In come the animals two by two
The lion ran and the dragons flew.
In come the animals three by three
In came the tiger and a bee.
In come the animals four by four
The kangaroo jumped and the rhino bashed the door.
In come the animals five by five
Some monkeys were dead and some were alive.
In come the animals six by six
Some learned tricks and some learned kicks.
In come the animals seven by seven
Lions stayed alive and some died.
In come the animals eight by eight
Some were early and some were late.

Christopher Wills (7)
Carniny Primary School

The Animal Poem

In come the animals two by two
The sheep went *baa* and the cows went *moo*.
In come the animals three by three
There were bees and monkeys in a tree.
In come the animals four by four
Birds through the window, elephants through the door.
In come the animals five by five
Some passed the garden, some passed the drive.
In come the animals six by six
They threw out the monkey because of its tricks.
In come the animals seven by seven
The very big lion thought he was going to Heaven.
In come the animals eight by eight
The billy goat went through the gate.

Ryan Douds (7)
Carniny Primary School

In Come The Animals

In come the animals two by two
In came the cows and they went *moo*
In come the animals three by three
The monkeys climbed down the tree
In come the animals four by four
The elephant smashed through the door
In come the animals five by five
The giraffe was half alive
In come the animals six by six
In came the beavers carrying sticks
In come the animals seven by seven
In came the dog and he was called Kevin
In come the animals eight by eight
The snake slithered on the plate.

Richard McCully (7)
Carniny Primary School

Young Writers - Once Upon A Rhyme Ballymena

In Come The Animals

In come the animals two by two
The elephants went *boo* and the monkeys went *whoo.*
In come the animals three by three
The monkey was a he and climbed a tree.
In come the animals four by four
Some hopped and some roared.
In come the animals five by five
The birds died and the hive was alive.
In come the animals six by six
Some played with sticks and some learned how to kick.
In come the animals seven by seven
One was eleven and went to Heaven.
In come the animals eight by eight
Some arrived early and some arrived late.

Sarah Fullerton (7)
Carniny Primary School

The Animal Poem

In come the animals two by two,
The cow went *moo* and the monkey went *boo.*
In come the animals three by three,
One had tea and one had me!
In come the animals four by four,
One had a floor and one had a mower.
In come the animals five by five,
One was alive and one was in the drive.
In come the animals six by six,
Dogs have sticks and cats have ticks.
In come the animals seven by seven,
Some were good and went to Heaven.
In come the animals eight by eight,
The snails were slower.

Neil McCluney (7)
Carniny Primary School

The People Poem

In come the boys one by one,
Some were smart and some were dumb.
In come the girls two by two,
Some said *boo* and some said *moo*.
In come the teachers three by three,
Some saw a bee and some drank tea.
In come the mummies four by four,
Some were slow and some were slower.
In come the hockey players five by five,
Some were alive and some had died.
In come the babies six by six,
Some have sticks and some need to be fixed.
In come the skateboarders seven by seven,
One was eleven and one was in Heaven.
In come the grandads eight by eight,
Some were early and some were late.

Mark Ramsey (8)
Carniny Primary School

Pecking Birds

P is for penguins running on the ice
E is for enormous owls in the night
C is for crows standing up tall
K is for kiwis trying not to fall
I   is for intelligent birds full of glee
N Is for nice, pretty birds up in the tree
G is for gorgeous birds in the sky

B is for birds who love to fly
I   is for indoor birds who like to rest
R is for robins with a red breast
D is for dirty birds who need a bath
S is for silly birds who like to laugh.

Jenny Sutherland (8)
Carniny Primary School

Young Writers - Once Upon A Rhyme Ballymena

The People Poem

In come the boys one by one
One was hungry and the other ate a bun.
In come the girls two by two
One was silly and one said boo.
In come the hockey players three by three
One got stung and the other likes bees.
In come the dancers four by four
One likes pigs and the other likes boars.
In come the swimmers five by five
One likes trees and the other likes hives.
In come the skateboarders six by six
One was silly and one does tricks.
In come the babies seven by seven
One was bad and the rest will go to Heaven.
In come the grandads eight by eight
One was early and the rest were late.

Sarah Kelso (8)
Carniny Primary School

Pecking Birds

P is for parrots that like to play ball
E is for eagles playing with a doll
C is for chicks standing so small
K is for kiwis trying to fall
I is for an igloo living with the Eskimo
N is for northern mocking bird singing a solo
G is for great reed warbler walking on the farm
B is for barn owl sitting in a barn
I is for interesting songbirds
R is for robin and its red breast
D is for dicky birds trying to bake
S is for swans swimming in the lake.

Kirsty McDowell (8)
Carniny Primary School

The People Poem

In come the boys two by two
One said boo and one said *boo!*
In come the girls three by three
And one hit her knee.
In come the teachers four by four
One let out a big roar.
In come the mummies five by five
One had died and one had lied.
In come the daddies six by six
One got in a mix.
In come the grannies seven by seven
One had a grandson called Kevin.
In come the grandads eight by eight
Some were early and some were late.
In come the babies nine by nine
One was hanging on a line.
In come the brides ten by ten
One had a pencil and one had a pen.
In come the grooms eleven by eleven
One died and went to Heaven.

Ben McCandless (8)
Carniny Primary School

School

S is for sums on the wall
C is for coats in the hall
H is for Miss Hamilton very tall
O is for orange paper on the wall
O is for outside playing with a ball
L is for Lyndsay in the hall.

Megan Campbell (7)
Carniny Primary School

The People Poem

In come the girls one by one,
One was silly, the other was dumb.
In come the boys two by two,
One said boo and the other said moo.
In come the mummies three by three,
One climbed a tree and the other had a sore knee.
In come the daddies four by four,
One came in the door and the other came in by the shore.
In come the grannies five by five,
One did a dive and the other can drive.
In come the tennis players six by six,
My dog licks and picks sticks.
In come the grandads seven by seven,
One was called Kevin and the other was called Evan.
In come the teachers eight by eight,
One came in the gate and the other ate off a plate.

Laura McCullough (8)
Carniny Primary School

My Dad

His hair is like patches of hair,
But he is really cool.
He has got bright blue eyes,
He loves music but he's really, really cool.
He wears a leather jacket sometimes
And always smells nice.
He has very hairy arms
And he has a big mouth.
Sometimes he is a cross bear,
But I just don't care!

Christopher Dalrymple (11)
Carniny Primary School

Hallowe'en

Scary monsters come out at night,
Waiting for you to start a fight.
Spooky witches with pointy hats,
Who have little, sweet black cats.

Fireworks going up and down,
And the Catherine wheel goes round and round.
So many colours for you to see,
The red ones are the colour for me.

Freaky skeletons armoured in bone,
And the ghosts all start to moan.
Can you guess which day I mean?
Yes, you're right, it's *Hallowe'en!*

Zoë McLees (11)
Carniny Primary School

The Scarecrow

S is for sun shining on the scarecrow tall
C is for crows chirping on the wall
A is for an army of scarecrows shooting
R is for rods and scarecrows fishing
E is for Eskimos making scarecrows in the snow
C is for clown scarecrows in a circus show
R is for rowing a boat down the stream
O is for obedient scarecrows and some are mean
W is for wasps and birds around the scarecrow scene.

Paul Johnston (8)
Carniny Primary School

Christmas

Christmas is a lovely time,
A time when you get presents
And you eat food.
It's a special time of year
Because Jesus Christ was born.
We celebrate His birth
And think of the shepherds and wise men.
We put up a tree
And decorate it with tinsel, baubles and lights.
We put up stockings
And wait for Santa Claus to come
And leave us presents.
We also give presents
And eat pudding and pie.
It's a very festive season.

Zach Templeton (10)
Carniny Primary School

The Scarecrow

S is for the sun shining on the wall
C is for coats flapping up tall
A is for an army of scarecrows
R is for scarecrows fishing by the pond
E is for birds eating the seeds
C is for a field of corn
R is for the rain all day long
O is for a scarecrow eating an orange
W is for the windy weather.

Peter Rodgers (8)
Carniny Primary School

The Wind

I can get through a doorway
without any key,
and strip the leaves
from the great oak tree.

I can blow off that
old man's favourite hat,
and send a gale force wind
through the lady's flat.

I can make that
wooden door slam,
and blow away
the girl's lip balm.

I can send shivers
through the boy's spine,
and blow that dust
to make the table shine.

Christie Law (10)
Carniny Primary School

School

S is for sums going round and round
C is for chasing each other in the playground
H is for hopping in PE
O is for opening up the book for me
O is for oranges in the hall
L is for lunch to eat after the bell.

Ryan Dowds (7)
Carniny Primary School

The Wind

If you're taking a penalty,
Beware of me.
If you want to know I'm there,
Look out the window and see.

In your bed,
Snug and warm,
Then suddenly there
Occurred a storm.

If there's a storm,
I'll be there,
If I waken you,
I don't care!

Christopher Quigley (10)
Carniny Primary School

Midnight Blue

Midnight blue,
Where are you?
Pipes cracking,
Mother yacking,
Granny knitting,
TV blaring,
I'm going down,
I'm very daring.

Christopher Cameron (11)
Carniny Primary School

Dragon

It swoops through the sky,
Almost too fast for the human eye.
'What is it, what do you think?'
Say sailors as they sink.
It does not know death,
It is the cause of death.
It is scaly, it is green,
It's hard to be seen.
It's large, it's huge,
It's a dragon.

Mark Herbison (11)
Carniny Primary School

Hallowe'en

Walking through a haunted house,
Nothing stirring, not even a mouse.
Creaking floorboards as I walk,
I cannot hear anyone talk.

I see ghosts floating around,
They are not making a sound.
Witches' cauldrons bubbling mad,
I really want my dad.

Emma Rose (11)
Carniny Primary School

The Man In The Can

A boy lived beside the Bann,
He lived in a can,
He drank Lucozade,
And hit his head on a spade
And then he left the land!

Paul McCrory (10)
Carniny Primary School

Young Writers - Once Upon A Rhyme Ballymena

The Wind

I can get through a doorway,
Without any key,
And strip the leaves
From the great oak tree.

I can slide through nooks and crannies,
Also blow the leaves,
Maybe even
Uproot trees.

I can blow a gale force wind,
Even make a tidal wave,
When I do that,
I can fill a shore's cave.

I can send shivers over you
And also put your windows through,
If I can find something to do,
It would be to blow the hat off you!

Connor Worthington (9)
Carniny Primary School

Vampires

White faces, scary cloaks lurking in the dark,
Wherever they are, they look for blood,
Always on the hunt,
They fly, they swoop to their kingdom high.

Their teeth are like metal spikes,
Their strength is unbelievable,
They run as fast as a Concorde plane
And they creep and lurk in sparkling dark.

Clinton McKeown (11)
Carniny Primary School

The Sea

The bubbling foam hits my toes,
The tiny grains hurt my feet,
Seagulls gliding through the air,
Sunshine lies on the sea.

The salty smell of the sea,
Bubbly, blue-white, glittering sea,
Jellyfish resting on the warm sand,
Dolphins jumping high,
If the rain comes on, it's all over.

Nichola Kennedy (11)
Carniny Primary School

Bullying

Up against the wall,
You seem very small,
As the other person seems very tall
And you feel like a toy doll.

You lose your pride,
As you're being pushed from side to side.

Gemma Jackson (12)
Carniny Primary School

What Is Winter?

Winter is snow, rain,
Sleet glistening,
Grass, iced ponds
And the cold breeze.
This is what winter feels like
To me!

Samantha Lowry (11)
Carniny Primary School

The Wind

I can whistle through doors
And blow down holes.
I lift off hats
And knock down poles.

I can sway ships from side to side,
I create waves in the water,
I send a shiver down your spine
And perhaps wake up an otter!

Matthew O'Neill (9)
Carniny Primary School

An Autumn Riddle

I wait in the tree for the wind,
I explode open,
I look like an egg,
I come on an evergreen tree,
My tree grows in parks.
What am I?

Answer: a pine cone.

Marc Law (10)
Carniny Primary School

The Wind

I can send shivers
Down your spine,
And blow leaves off trees
To make a line.

I can make your curtains flutter
And even make your hat shutter.
I can whistle to your cat
And blow away every rat!

Lauren Davison (10)
Carniny Primary School

Ballymena

Ballymena, the town of the seven towers,
There are lots of important places around us,
Like the leisure centre and the Adair Arms.

The Ecos Centre is where we like to be,
With science and technology,
And things we like to do and see.

The Saturday Fairhill market,
Is almost a thing of the past,
Because now you can shop really fast!

Steven Carruthers (10)
Carniny Primary School

An Autumn Riddle

I wait for the wind,
I wait for the crash. Bang!
Been inside all spring and summer,
It's too warm,
Then I open up, I'm free,
I get out of my prickly shell,
At last I say to myself,
Here comes the flights,
What am I?

Hannah Mckillop (9)
Carniny Primary School

How Other People See Me

To my parents I am a terror,
To my brother I am fun,
To my neighbours I am annoying,
To my teacher I am brainy,
To my friends I am crazy,
But to myself I am just me!

Jack Murray (9)
Carniny Primary School

Young Writers - Once Upon A Rhyme Ballymena

The Wind

I can uproot a tree
Without any spade,
And make a
Mammoth of a wave.

I can scatter leaves
Along the ground,
And blow a ball
Out of any playground.

I can send shivers
Down your spine,
As you queue up outside the bank
Waiting in a line.

Leah Wright (10)
Carniny Primary School

Diamond Trail

As a firework takes off,
It looks like a magnum waterfall,
Flying round the sky,
With an array of colours,
The sounds of a Concorde,
Cruising at mach 2,
It looks like the aurora borealis,
The feel of an untouchable light,
Sounds like a Concorde's cabin,
. . . De-pressurising.

Simon Boyd (10)
Carniny Primary School

The Wind

I can get through a doorway
Without any key
And strip the leaves
From the great oak tree.

I can blow so hard and make things fly
And drive the clouds across the sky
The birds won't fly and cats will flee
Everyone is afraid of me.

I can blow off your hat
And make it fly away
And make your children shiver
All through the day.

Robbie Sutherland (9)
Carniny Primary School

The Victorious Vikings

They came in their huge longboats,
To take our gold and riches,
To sell us into slavery
And put us in the ditches.

They came from Scandinavia,
To roam across our land,
And burn the monks' monasteries
Right down, till thoy looked like sand.

Nicolle Scroggie (10)
Carniny Primary School

Whiz Wheels

Whoosh! Whiz!
A flame, a spark!
The Catherine wheel spins in the dark,
A shower of flames,
A scarf of smoke,
A wailing pig's speech,
A barn owl's screech,
A blazing furnace,
A round volcano,
Round and round,
A round volcano.

A spinning shower
With machine gun power,
Loud as a lion,
Big as Orion,
Fast as a cheetah,
A round volcano,
Round and round,
A round volcano.

Kimberley Carmichael (9)
Carniny Primary School

Fireworks

As the fireworks went shooting up,
Like a colourful shooting star,
Then split into little lights
And came down like a waterfall.

They sounded as if a bomb went off,
Or a baby screaming loud,
It was as hot as a burning fire,
Or the sun beating down.

Lauren Neilly (9)
Carniny Primary School

Furry Friend?

I don't like rats,
But I really love cats
And I'm quite undecided
About little brown bats.

They're really quite timid,
Their eyesight isn't good,
And they don't go to bed
When everyone should.

They don't stand up,
But hang upside down,
And they're hard to see
Because they're usually brown.

Milk is what they like to drink,
And bats can hear things we can't,
            I think!

Lauren McNair   (9)
Carniny Primary School

The Wind

I can send gale force winds,
With a kick,
When you're on a boat,
I can make you sick.

I can send a super blow
Which is bitterly cold,
I move big waves,
Over the sand so gold.

Stephen Leetch   (9)
Carniny Primary School

How Other People See Me

To my parents I'm very lively,
To my brothers I'm incredibly annoying,
To my neighbours I'm just fine,
To my friends I'm crazy and mad,
To my teacher I'm a well-behaved girl,
To my granny and grandad I'm a bit cheeky,
To my cousins I'm very happy and bright,
To my aunt and uncle I'm an angel,
But to myself I'm just me!

Kelly McCloy (9)
Carniny Primary School

Cats

Cats sleep,
They eat cat food,
They kill mice and maybe birds,
Miaow.

Matthew Booth (10)
Carniny Primary School

How Other People See Me

To my parents I'm hysterical and quite untidy,
To my brother I'm double trouble,
To my neighbours I'm just a little pest,
To my friends I'm cool and humorous,
To my teacher I'm quite chatty but I'm a steady worker,
But to myself I'm just me!

Gillian Hutchinson (9)
Carniny Primary School

Fireworks

Rockets . . .
Look like a baby's drawing of scribbles,
Sound like screaming children,
Like an army bomb, but louder,
Feels like a helicopter taking off,
Looks like a bursting fire in the air
And appears like a waterfall trickling down.

Joel Scullion (10)
Carniny Primary School

The Car Rhyme

Once there were two boys
Named Rome and Bryan.
They both had two cars
Which came from Mars.

Then they met two boys
Named Jimmy and Taz.
They also had two cars
But were not from Mars.

Bryan's neon was yellow
When he was under a pillow.
Rome's was red
When he had a head.

Jimmy's neon was blue
When he was two.
Taz's was green.

Carl Sloan (10)
Kells And Connor Primary School

Dolphin Daydream

Once upon a time
I thought of a rhyme
About a daydream.

I was near a pretty lagoon
When I saw an ugly baboon
Which was pointing at . . .
A friendly dolphin.

It flipped, it dived
It swam in circles very fast
Then at last it stopped
Right in front of the baboon.

The dolphin talked to me
The baboon walked towards me
And said, 'Hop on the dolphin's back
Take a trip back in time.'

So I said I would
But wondered if I could . . .
Go back in time.

I saw myself in the past
Then I saw my mum, at last!
'I miss her,' I said to the dolphin.
So he took me home
Said hello to my mum and left.

Gemma Scott (10)
Kells And Connor Primary School

Cars

They are fast, they're furious and they're serious
They're cool and they rule
They're bad and they are fabulous all together
The tools are behind the fuel tanks
Are they from Mars or are they
Just regular cars?

Michael Davidson (9)
Kells And Connor Primary School

Slow Beats Fast

A Ford Escort and a MX270 tractor
They wanted to have a race at a faraway place
So they went to Kells, they went to Connor
But not a place could they find.

They gave up and went to dine
And it was fine.
So they went to bed with teddy bear Ted
Teddy bear Ted came with a car and a candy bar.

The next morning they woke
And they went to Ballymena and the arena
Then they found a place outside of Ballymena
And got the race ready for the next day.

The next day when someone said go
The Ford rocketed on while the tractor went slow
The Ford at 200mph
The tractor only 30.

But the Ford was so fast it had blown up the engine
And the tractor went slowly by and won
And out came the sun.

Jonathan Erwin (9)
Kells And Connor Primary School

School

One morning as I was walking up the school path,
I heard a voice shout, 'Come on you little lass.'
I looked up and saw Miss Porter and said,
'I won't be late for class.'

Then I went into the classroom and said,
'Good morning boys and girls.'
Pencils at the ready, let's get our school work done
And then when the bell rings, it's time for lots of fun.

Edwina Taylor (10)
Kells And Connor Primary School

Football

Football is a game of skill
A game of strength and might
So if you lose don't start to fight

David became a football star
A football star and legend
So I'd just try and do your best
And save the rest for later

Manchester Utd are my favourite team
And Real Madrid are my second
Leeds Utd are really bad
That's what I reckon

David is a free kick taker
And most of the time he scores
But my favourite player is Mols
And he is from Rangers

Ronaldo is a top goal scorer
As he won the golden boot
But it was a fluke.

Richard French (9)
Kells And Connor Primary School

Lilly Being Silly

Once upon a time
Upon a crime
To sit in school
To write a poem
About a stone
To have it published
In the paper.

I feel so silly
To be called Lilly
I can't wait to get home
'Cause I feel so silly.

Anthony Craig (10)
Kells And Connor Primary School

History

The Romans are red
The Vikings are blue
The Saxons are happy
But we are one short of a crew.

Odin's a chief
But also a thief
And Thor eats more than a boar
But when he hits you it's very sore
And goes right down to the core.

When giants stole Thor's hammer
They made a big mistake
And all of a sudden they were made into
Cake.

H orrible
I nteresting
S ick
T errible
O dd
R ough
Y ucky

That's the way I describe history
Horrible.

John Mawhinney (9)
Kells And Connor Primary School

Creatures Of The Sea

I wish, oh I wish,
I could see the seaside sea,
The dolphins, the penguins
And the seagulls I see.

Oh, what a pity,
For the creatures I see,
Because they are going to sea.

I go out on a boat to find where they float,
Because I'm so fierce,
I might get soaked.

So listen to this,
Don't dump your waste
On the seaside place,
The animals will get poisoned.

S unny,
E xciting,
A mazing,
S and,
I ce cream,
D elicate,
S E agulls.

Samantha Magill (10)
Kells And Connor Primary School

Ice Cream

Ice cream, ice cream
Nice and cold.

Ice cream, ice cream
With a cone.

Ice cream, ice cream
With sprinkles and marshmallows.

Ice cream, ice cream
Eaten by the hallows.

Ice cream, ice cream
With chocolate sauce.

Ice cream, ice cream
With some floss.

Ice cream, ice cream
With a flake.

Ice cream, ice cream
With a free cake.

Ice cream, ice cream
My dad takes one.

Ice cream, ice cream
I get a free bun.

Mark Smyth (9)
Kells And Connor Primary School

Boys

Do you wish that boys could be more like girls?
You know what girls are like -
Pretty, smart and kind.
But you don't know what boys are like -
Big-headed, silly and stupid.
I agree that boys are one of a kind.
I am fed up with boys to the tip of my head,
To the last layer of skin and the back of my leg.
If I have to sit in-between two boys,
I will jump straight out the window.
If I had powers, I would turn all boys into girls,
So you'd better watch out! I'll be invisible as well!

What do you think? You tell me.

Emma Hutchinson (9)
Kells And Connor Primary School

Roxy's Sleepover

S lumber parties are fun,
L izzy tells jokes and boy, they're funny,
E njoy listening to each other's secrets,
E ven have some pillow fights,
P lay with groovy games,
O ften do funky make-overs,
V icky will bring some tasty treats,
E ven sing on a karaoke machine,
R oxy will show us some foxy styles,
S tacy will tell scary ghost stories in the dark!
    Boo!

Rachel Martin (10)
Kells And Connor Primary School

Cars

I have a car, it's a very powerful car
It zooms up the road
Sometimes carrying a very heavy load.
The windows shine all the time
And the engine roars like a boar
And the neon is positively not in sight
But makes it zoom fast in the night.
When the race is starting
We make our parting flying down the road.
The eyes they glare as the engines flare
The cheers they echo through the air
Everyone's excited
The atmosphere is clear
And that's how my car
Went so far.

Colin Price (9)
Kells And Connor Primary School

A World Of Dogs

Anything that moves chase it
In his eyes the sparkle must never end
Remembering the world is to protect
His heart is as big as any other dog's.

Looking over the world
Seeing who is bad
Now he has a bundle of pups
They will be just like their dad.

A reward well done
A life-saving rescue
Smelling a scent all the time
A race has no finish line
He says there is no such thing as a bad weather day
Is it true?

Rebecca Feeney (10)
Kells And Connor Primary School

School

Children are silent and bright
In the mornings.
Computers are fascinating, enormous.
The teachers have sunny, bright faces
And funny, runny noses.
Most of the teachers' ears are like
Bunny ears, some children
Fistle at papers.
There are games that James and John
Play with and girls sometimes play with
Games but James plays with boys' games.
He hides them so that no one will get them.

The teachers shout, *'Wake up, you're sleeping!'*
In the dinner hall they are fast, last
And blast the dinner plates.
All in the dinner hall the servers are fast.

Kim White (10)
Kells And Connor Primary School

Winter

Winter, it's boring
Until the snow comes
We can blow it away with a snow blower
Or throw it at our friends
It is a lot of fun, especially once Christmas comes
We can run down the stairs
And rip the paper off our presents
Or when I get £100 from my dad
It is a lot of fun when we can slide about on the ice
But it's not so much fun when we fall on our backside
Then the snow melts and it's back to plain old winter.

Jonathan Caldwell (10)
Kells And Connor Primary School

Candy Treats

Candy is a sweet
We get it as a treat
Candy can be chocolate
White, dark or brown.

Toffee which is sticky and sweet
Rainbow drops are bright
Everlasting gob-stoppers never stop
Alien avalanches erupt
Thick chocolate melts away
Scrumpdidlyumptious sweets.

Candy treats
Are fun to eat
So take my advice
They're very, very sweet.

Bethany Brown (9)
Kells And Connor Primary School

Burgers

I am called Morris
But some people call me Doris.

I love burgers
They are my favourite food.
I go down to Burger King
And get one for my tea.

But watch out!
If you eat too many
They'll certainly make you fat.

I went home and told my mum
My favourite food was burgers.
She said, 'They might be nice
But don't go there tomorrow
Or you'll be as fat as a cat!'

Samuel McIlveen (9)
Kells And Connor Primary School

My World

It looks like paradise
With flowers blooming everywhere
And the waterfalls flowing with orange juice

You can hear only happy voices and animals
As peace flows throughout the land
No gunshots or cries for help
Just peace and kindness

You can only smell barbecues
And taste treats for everyone to enjoy
It tastes like everything you have ever wanted
Instead of leaves, my trees grow sweets
Fruit and whatever else you wish for

And there is one thing for sure
My world feels great and you can do whatever you want
Whenever you want and no one
Can push you around because it is
My world for all to share.

Gemma Dickey (11)
Longstone Primary School

Poem

I, Tamara Marshall
A girl, smart, talented and thin
Daughter of Colin and Jacqueline Marshall
Sister of Tiffany, Colin and Ronnie Marshall
Who feels happy when with the best friend in the world
Who fears being alone in the darkest of nights after having
nightmares
Who would like to see a world with no pain and no sorrow
Am a resident of Randalstown
Welcome you to my poem.

Tamara Marshall (9)
Longstone Primary School

My World Poem

I wish my world could be noisy,
There would be whatever I want.
There would be drinks, sweets,
Everything I could wish for, and no more panicking.

I wish my world could be made of chocolate,
When you eat, the chocolate would come back again,
And there would be more every time,
Oh, I just wish that could happen.

I wish there would never be worries again.

Jonathan Kerr (8)
Longstone Primary School

Poem

I, Robynne Cameron
A girl, funny, happy and joyful
Daughter of David and Florence
Sister of Marc
Who feels happy with my family and friends
Who fears nightmares in the dark
Who would like to see a world with no pain
A resident of Ahoghill
Welcome you to my poem.

Robynne Cameron (9)
Longstone Primary School

My World

I dream of my world to be perfect
A chocolate milk swimming pool
It smells like nice, smooth, melting chocolate
The mountains taste like spicy pepper
The houses are made out of fluffy candyfloss
You can feel a lovely, smooth, furry cat.

Nathan Dickey (9)
Longstone Primary School

Poem

I, Jack Johnston
A boy, smart, funny and rough
Son of Harry and Helen
Brother of Mark and Richard
Who feels glad behind a map on holiday
Who fears when our neighbour's dog walks down to our house
Who would like to see everyone being friends every day
Am a resident of Ahoghill
Welcome you to my poem.

Jack Johnston (9)
Longstone Primary School

Poem

I, Samuel Finlay
A boy, smart, funny and thin
Son of Russell and Evelyn
Brother of no one
Who feels happy when Friday comes
Who fears jellyfish
Who would like to see a world of peace
Am a resident of Ahoghill
Welcome you to my poem.

Samuel Finlay (9)
Longstone Primary School

Winter

Winter is a time of year
When birds go far away
And the cold is here to stay
So we all can have some fun
Because there is no school.

Daniel McKillen (10)
Moorfields Primary School

The Farmyard

T he stillness of the morning was shattered
H orses neighing, cows mooing, pigs grunting
E ven the sheep wanted to be heard.

F armer John waited for the rooster's crow
A n alarm clock was not on the go
R ising early was no problem at all
M ilking cows was his first port of call
Y oung lambs were appearing in the fields
A nd birds were singing in the trees
R over the sheepdog is gently yawning
D ear me, he thinks, it can't be morning.

Stewart McIlwaine (10)
Moorfields Primary School

Teacher

T eacher, teacher, just go away
E ven when you're not there it seems like you
A re and I
C an't cope with another day working this
H ard. Oh teacher, just give us
E asier work or I wish you would
R ather let us play. Teacher, teacher, just go away.

Christine Freckingham (10)
Moorfields Primary School

Perfect Emma

I wish I was a queen,
Like Queen Emma in Norman times.
Tall, majestic, powerful - never gets detention!

I wish I had my friend Emma Steele's hair.
Strawberry blonde, straight - no curls!

I wish I could sing like Emma Bunton.
In tune, sweet - not like a frog!

I wish I had the complexion of Jane Austen's Emma.
Fair, flawless - not a pimple in sight.

I wish there were two of me,
Like Catherine Sefton's novel.
Just think of all the mischief I could get up to then!
Now wouldn't that be perfect, Emma?

Emma Dawson (10)
Moorfields Primary School

Animals

A nimals, I like them all
N o matter if they are big or small
I love them a lot for they play with me
M y family love them too
A n elephant to a flea
L ove is what an animal needs
S o treat them with respect.

Ruth Walker (11)
Moorfields Primary School

My Football Dreams

The day of the week I like the best
It must be Saturday above the rest.
As I get dressed, the excitement builds
For playing football with all its thrills.
In my new kit I look quite smart
And in and out I hope to dart.
Dribbling and tackling are quite a fine art
And when I hear the crowds all cheer
At Ibrox stadium I'll think, I'm here.
Until my mate shouts, 'Hey, Krissy Toal
You've put in a first class goal.'

Kristoffer Steele (11)
Moorfields Primary School

Moiles

M oiles are my favourite cattle
O rganising and grooming for the show
I rish moiles is the proper name
L eading them on the halter round the ring
E arly to bed, early to rise for the show
S houting with joy for the Irish moile came first!

David White (11)
Moorfields Primary School

Spring

Snowdrops form white beds
Crocuses raise their heads
Buds are beginning to appear
Spring will soon be here.

Lucinda Ellis (10)
Moorfields Primary School

Music

Music is my favourite thing,
There's lots of things to do,
In carol services I have to sing,
But there's other stuff too.

Well, there's the clarinet, violin, organ too,
A nice and calm flute,
Drums with piles of banging to do
And a trumpet so you can toot.

In piano I play a song,
The teacher tells me what to do,
The teacher tells me if I'm wrong
And how to correct it too.

In violin every week,
I play it at school,
The teacher says to play a tune
And says if it is cool.

Donna McCord (11)
Moorfields Primary School

Left Out

I'm left out.
I've got a baby brother and I know
How annoying they can be.
And it's not fair.
He gets what he wants
But I don't.
When he cries they all go rushing over
To see what the matter is
But they just say to me
'You'll be alright.'
And what's more, Mum says
I have to eat my greens but
My brother spits his out.
So I think that I'm left out.

Gemma Russell (10)
Moorfields Primary School

FIFA Football

F ootball is my favourite sport
I play it on the PC
F or all the players in the world
A re certain to agree,

F erdinand who plays for Ferguson
O r Ruud Van Nistleroy
O n the pitch and off the pitch, I'm sure their view's the same
T hat football is a clever game.
B all control and footie tricks
A re skills a player needs
L ast but most importantly
L eading our team to victory!

Andrew Ellison (11)
Moorfields Primary School

Skateboard

S is for skating which I do for a sport.
K is for kickflip which is a trick.
A is for Adio who sponsors pro skaters.
T is for trucks which are part of the board.
E is for extreme sports which I watch on the TV.
B is for Bam Magera who's my favourite skater
O is for Oink skateboards.
A is for airwalk which you can do on a half-pipe.
R is for rocket air which is a trick some pros can do.
D is for darkslide which you can do only on a rail.

Adam Brown (10)
Moorfields Primary School

Young Writers - Once Upon A Rhyme Ballymena

Beards

Beards are really funny things
They swirl around your chin
The only trouble with them is
They pick up bits of din.

Beards can keep you occupied
In many a different way
You can pass the time at bus stops
Finding food from yesterday.

Can a man survive without
A teddy bear in bed?
He can,
Oh yes, he can!
He grows a cuddly beard instead.

With patience and with practise
True style can be yours
From trendy, twirling goatee
To full-on Santa Claus.

When I'm as old as Dad
And have a beard of my own
I'll weave some seashells in it
And leave it overgrown.

Angus Gibson (11)
Moorfields Primary School

Pets

P ets are cute and cuddly,
E very day and night,
T oys they play with,
S oft, colourful and bright.

Laura Handley (10)
Moorfields Primary School

Scamp

She used to run and frolic
And rabbits she would chase,
But now she lies all curled up
With that tired look on her face.
At the slightest sound her ears would prick
And her eyes were bright like stars,
But now that sparkle has left those eyes
And her ears droop down so far.
Her glossy coat stays soft and smooth
Her nose now not so wet,
But inside that old girl's coat
Is still my lovable pet.
It doesn't matter that now she's old
I still love her so much,
Her friendly manner and cheerful ways
My heart will always touch.

Jonathan Nevin (11)
Moorfields Primary School

Sounds

I heard the sounds
Of the countryside,
Of birds and trees
All so perfectly at ease.

In other parts of the world
Bombs and bullets disturb the calm,
And we all wonder
Where has the peacefulness gone?

Rebecca Warwick (10)
Moorfields Primary School

Exams

Exams are tough!
Who says?
Everyone says.
Mum says study.
Dad says don't worry.
But now they're over,
Life's a daisy.
Time goes by
And I can be lazy.

Caleb Morrison (11)
Moorfields Primary School

Football

F ootball is great fun
O h, don't forget to use your skills
O h, don't forget to pass
T hat's how you score a goal
B e a player your coach can be proud of
A nd make sure you score and win the game or
L et your coach be proud or
L ose the game and your coach will be angry.

Aaron Cairns (10)
Moorfields Primary School

Portrait Of A Basilisk

For its head
I would use a snake's head
And the colour of dark trees.

For its body
I would borrow a long, slimy
Cobra from a zoo.

For its eyes
I would borrow hot, blazing
Fire in the cold.

For its teeth
I would use a sharp, silver
Sword from a dark knight.

For its mane
I would use a red, devilish
Colour which glows in the dark.

Darren McLaughlin (8)
St Mary's Primary School, Cushendall

Dogs

When I think of dogs
They make me laugh
Because they're good looking
Just like me.

Then I said to myself
Why don't I get one
Instead of dreaming of them?

Now I have one
And use it for hunting
And playing in parks and on the beach.

Sean McAfee (10)
St Mary's Primary School, Cushendall

Portrait Of A Unicorn

For his head
I'd use a
Pure white Arabian stallion.

For his body
I'd have a
Shimmering white cloud.

For his hooves
I'd borrow a
Black piece of coal.

For his tail
I'd use a river
Silver in the sun.

And for his horn
I'd need a
Sharp crystal, light-grey
Like the winter sun.

Cliodhna Maskey (8)
St Mary's Primary School, Cushendall

Portrait Of A Unicorn

For his head
I'd use a snowdrop-white Arabian.

For his hooves
I'd borrow starlight, sparkling diamonds.

For his body
I'd have a shimmering soft cloud.

For his tail
I'd use a glistening waterfall.

For his horn
I'd need a silver sharp sword.

Hannah McAlister (8)
St Mary's Primary School, Cushendall

Portrait Of A Unicorn

For his head
I'd use a snow-white
Arabian mare.

For his body
I'd have a soft, snowy
Cloud from the sky.

For his hooves
I'd borrow pure black
Sparkling stones from the beach.

For his tail
I'd use a silver waterfall
Flowing gracefully through the forest.

And for his horn
I'd need a sharp sword
Sparkling in the moonlight.

Sarah Morgan (8)
St Mary's Primary School, Cushendall

My Dream

Dominic Delargy is my name,
Football and hurling are my games.

Sometimes when I have a dream,
I am playing on the Antrim team.

All the people shout and roar,
When I make the final score.

With a hurling stick and a ball,
Up the Saffrons, up Cushendall.

Dominic Delargy (10)
St Mary's Primary School, Cushendall

Portrait Of A Unicorn

For her head
I'd have a snow-white Arabian mare,
From the deserts of Arabia.

For her body
I'd have a white, shimmering cloud,
From the Australian sky.

For her hooves
I'd borrow pure black coal,
From the deepest mines in Africa.

For her tail
I'd use silver moonlight
Caught in a net.

And for her horn
I'd need a sharp, silver sword,
From a very brave knight.

Soracha Cosgrove (9)
St Mary's Primary School, Cushendall

Horses And Ponies

H orses and ponies galloping away
O ver the fields they stray
R oaming freely into the sun
S topping for no one, on they run
E verywhere they go
S cattering the snow.

P layful and happy
O h, but not snappy
N othing but fun, the foals canter on
I nto the forests they make a trail
E vergreen trees protecting their way
S o no one knows how long they will stay.

Katie Bowen (10)
St Mary's Primary School, Cushendall

Portrait Of A Unicorn

For his head
I'd use a pure white
Horse's head.

For his body
I'd have a soft, white
Cloud.

For his hooves
I'd borrow four
Jet-black
Stones.

For his tail
I'd use a sparkling
Waterfall flowing
Into a river.

And for his horn
I'd need a giant pointed thorn
Shining silvery-white in
The sun.

Eoin McManus (8)
St Mary's Primary School, Cushendall

Snooker

I was playing snooker
The cue ball hit the cooker

When we were playing our game
My brother won the first frame.

Eoghan Allen (9)
St Mary's Primary School, Cushendall

Portrait Of A Basilisk

For his head
I'd use
The dark green leaves of a pine tree.

For the tail
I'd borrow
A dark green python
Slithering through the Amazon jungle.

For his teeth
I'd need
The starlight silver
Of hundreds of the sharpest swords.

But I'd save
The best for last.
For his dangerous eyes
I'd use
The volcano red
Mixed with the crocus yellow
And marigold orange.

Paul McCurry (8)
St Mary's Primary School, Cushendall

My Big Brother

My big brother is so annoying
He didn't finish off his drawing
He comes and says, 'You're a pest'
While all he does is rest
And everyone else is doing their best
To sort out the mess him and his friends have left.

Leanne McKeegan (10)
St Mary's Primary School, Cushendall

Portrait Of A Unicorn

For his head
I'd use a snow-white
Arabian stallion.

For his body
I'd have a fluffy
White cloud
Pulled from the sky.

For his hooves
I'd borrow sparkling
Black stones
Gathered from the beach.

For his tail
I'd use a glittery
Silver waterfall flowing
Over a cliff.

And for his horn
I'd need an ice sword
Shining with starlight
In a clear night.

Fiona Rowan (9)
St Mary's Primary School, Cushendall

My First Day At School

My first day at school was so cool
I bought some new pens and made friends
The sky was blue
And the sun was out too
I had no homework and that was great
After that I walked home with my best mate.

Clare Morgan (10)
St Mary's Primary School, Cushendall

Portrait Of A Basilisk

For its head
I'd use a
Snake's head, forest green.

For its body
I'd borrow a
Long, slimy python
From our local zoo.

For its eyes
I'd have
Two hot lumps
Of blazing lava.

For its teeth
I'd use
Pure white icicles
From Antarctica.

For its hair
I'd use a
Red stallion's mane
From Saudi Arabia.

Shaun O'Boyle (9)
St Mary's Primary School, Cushendall

My Dad's Ship

My dad's ship is very large,
It's one hundred thousand ton,
It travels at a speed of thirty knots.
Today Dad phoned from the Indian Ocean,
He's on his way to Sri Lanka
And the temperature is thirty-two degrees.
I miss my dad.

Patrick Blaney (10)
St Mary's Primary School, Cushendall

Portrait Of A Unicorn

For his head
I'd use a pure
White stallion.

For his body
I'd have a snowy
Soft cloud.

For his hooves
I'd borrow pure
Black coal.

For his tail
I'd use a silver
Shining waterfall.

And for his horn
I'd need a sharp
Silver sword.

Alex Delargy (8)
St Mary's Primary School, Cushendall

Amie

My little sister, Amie
Is very, very good
She always tidies up her room
And eats up all her food.
When Mum takes the shopping home
She helps unpack the car
Then she opens up the biscuits
And she has a chocolate bar.

Sarah Callaghan (9)
St Mary's Primary School, Cushendall

The Holidays

The holidays aren't boring,
There's a cat sleeping happily in the sun,
I think he's snoring,
I want a nice cream bun.

I'll go to the pool
And get all wet,
The girls said my party was cool
And they helped me pick my very first pet.

The holidays become very hot,
I'll put on this T-shirt,
I want to go for a walk, not,
I'll put on these shoes and maybe this top.

I'll lie on the grass
And get a nice tan,
I'll get my sister to do everything for me - class,
I'll tell her to get me a fan.

This is the best holiday of all,
Everyone is having fun,
Let's go out and play some ball,
It doesn't feel like one day's gone by, not one.

At the end of the holidays we go back to school,
I'll get a new lunch bag and some trainers too,
My new school bag is cool,
I've forgotten my pens, I'm such a fool.

On the day before school,
I'll tidy my room,
I've broken some clips, I'm such a fool,
I'll sweep the floor with a broom.

Before I go to bed tonight,
I'll read a few pages of a book
And I'll give my brother a little fright,
When I go into my room I'll put my dressing gown on its hook.

I'll climb into bed and say my prayers,
I'll turn out the lights and close my eyes,
The holidays will be back next year
And we can have fun again.

Caoimhe McManus (10)
St Mary's Primary School, Cushendall

Who Are These People?

These people always help me out,
They never show a pout.

These people put a roof over my head
And give me a nice warm bed.

These people are *so* good to me,
They also taught me to swim in the sea.

These people take me different places,
They taught me how to tie my shoelaces.

These people make sure I'm alright,
If I have a sting or insect bite.

These people cook food for me,
Then afterwards we have cups of tea.

These people taught me good from bad,
They help me if I'm feeling sad.

These people love me very dearly
And I love them just as sincerely.

Kathryn McIlroy (9)
St Mary's Primary School, Cushendall

My Twin Brother

I have a twin brother
Stephen is his name
Getting up to mischief is his silly game

He stands behind the door
Waiting for footsteps on the wooden floor
Then pounces like a cat
As if his victim were a rat

He thinks it is so funny
But no one seems to laugh
It makes me feel so stupid
To be his other half

Some people say he is a rascal
Others say he is a pup
But he is my little brother
So I think I've said enough.

Leona McAuley (9)
St Mary's Primary School, Cushendall

Sure That's What Friends Are For

My friend, she means so much to me
As much as my own family.
When I am hurt or feeling glum
She always is the first to come
To help me get back on my feet
She is the best mate you could meet.

And if I thought she was in trouble
I'd be right round at the double
To see what I could do for her . . .
Sure, isn't that what friends are for?

Moira Molloy (10)
St Mary's Primary School, Cushendall

My Big Sister

My big sister is so daft
She said, 'You look funny doing craft'
I said, 'Shove off and go away'
She won't even leave me to play
I try to ignore her
But no, no, no
She just won't leave me alone
She stuck on perfume and dressed up nice
Then she came into my room
She giggled under her breath, 'Hee, hee, hee'
I said, 'Why did it have to be me, me, me?'
Oh, why do I have a big sister
'Blaa, blaa, blaa,' I said to her
I told my mum to tell her off
But at the time she was whispering
'It's Maltesers I like to scoff'
I said, 'Buzz off.'

Declan McAlister (9)
St Mary's Primary School, Cushendall

The Headmaster's Warning

One, two, you boy, yes I'm talking to you
Three, four, stop hitting that floor
Five, six, don't be playing those tricks
Seven, eight, come back, don't be late
Nine, ten, OK, but don't be bad then
Eleven, twelve, be like myself
Thirteen, fourteen, if you do something bad you'll be seen
Fifteen, sixteen, come back after school
Seventeen, eighteen, stop that eating
Nineteen, twenty, that's a pity, you've done plenty.

Andrew Delargy (10)
St Mary's Primary School, Cushendall

Football

I thought I was good
But nobody said, 'Go dude'
Except for those boys
Who still play with their toys
They are twelve but act
Like two, that's a fact
I thought the crowd said, 'Go gnome'
But they really said, 'Go home'
My mum said I was a wonder
My dad said I was a blunder.

Next Sunday it was a different story
The crowd chanted, 'Corry! Corry!'
I thought it was me they were talking to
But when I looked at them they started walking home
Then I let in a goal and they all went home
After the match everybody said, 'Doh! Gnome!'

Next Sunday I was doing nets
People were placing bets
That I would let in ten
I felt like hiding in a den
Because I let in one goal . . .
Per minute. My excuse was the ball hit a hole
And it went over my head
The manager said, 'You're dead, Corry Gnome.'

Conor McAlister (10)
St Mary's Primary School, Cushendall

An Only Son

I have four sisters
The youngest is a brat
She brings me out in blisters
And attacks me like a cat

When I think of all the others
Monsters spring to mind
They roar and shout
And mess me about
Oh God! I can't wait to put them out

My dad just sits there like a mouse
As they all try to wreck the house
Mum is in the middle
And I'm as fit as a fiddle
Such fun to see them cross
But girls remember, I am boss.

Stephen McAuley (9)
St Mary's Primary School, Cushendall

Farm Animals

When I think of farm animals,
I think they are quite good.
But then I know something
Thoy do is quite rude.
Oh, farm animals, farm animals
They are like them man animals.

But if only they knew how to do gymnastics,
It would make them more fantastic.

Maria Kane (9)
St Mary's Primary School, Cushendall

The Sea

The sea can roar,
The sea can howl,
The sea can crash,
Like an angry wolf's growl.

The sea can be calm,
The sea can be cool,
The sea can be soft,
Like sheep's wool.

Caolan Diamond (7)
St Mary's Primary School, Greenlough

The Sea

The sea can dip,
The sea can crash,
The sea can grip,
Like a bear in a cage.

The sea can be wavy,
The sea can whisper,
The sea can be caring,
Like a quiet cat.

Michael Henry (8)
St Mary's Primary School, Greenlough

The Sea

The sea can roar,
The sea can rage,
The sea can growl,
Like a large bear in a cage.

The sea can splash,
The sea can freeze,
The sea can cool,
Like a gentle breeze.

Ryan McGoldrick (8)
St Mary's Primary School, Greenlough

The Sea

The sea can rip,
The sea can bash,
The sea can bang,
Like a giant crash.

The sea can be peaceful,
The sea can be cool,
The sea can be soft,
Like a sheep's wool.

Erin O'Neill (8)
St Mary's Primary School, Greenlough

The Sea

The sea can tip
The sea can growl
The sea can grip
Like a tiger on the prowl.

The sea can be kind
The sea can be flat
The sea can be careful
Like a very slow cat.

Paul Carey (8)
St Mary's Primary School, Greenlough

The Sea

The sea can tumble,
The sea can tear,
The sea can rip,
Like an angry bear.

The sea can be gentle,
The sea can be cool,
The sea can be flat,
Like a giant pool.

Niall Loughlin (8)
St Mary's Primary School, Greenlough

Star Shapes

A star is a gentle eye
Sparkling up in the sky.

A star is a snowflake oh so very cold
And then it is brightened by some magic gold.

A star is a jewel on a crown
And an angel can always wear it and look down.

A star is a silver fish
Swimming in a blue dish.

Aimee Cassidy (8)
St Mary's Primary School, Greenlough

Star Shapes

A star is like a beautiful feather
Floating on a large piece of treasure.

A star is like a singing dove
Like a bright hole of love.

A star is like a spying eye
When the moon floods the sky.

A star is like a tiny white dot
When the moonlight hits the spot.

Seanin Marron (8)
St Mary's Primary School, Greenlough

Star Shapes

A star is a teardrop dripping down a face
A star is treasure shining in space.

A star is an angel peeking through a hole
A star is a snowflake floating down so cold.

A star is a ring shining on the finger of a king
A star is a feather diamond on a dove's wing.

Emma Mooney (7)
St Mary's Primary School, Greenlough

Star Shapes

A star is like a fish swimming round moon's house.
A star is like a gentle cat swiping at a mouse.

A star is like a white monkey swinging round and round.
A star is like a new pupil going out of bounds.

A star is like an astronaut walking on the moon.
A star is like a peaceful owl coming in at noon.

A star is like a grey mouse scurrying everywhere.
A star is like a feathery dove flying in mid-air.

Breandán McNally (8)
St Mary's Primary School, Greenlough

Star Shapes

A star is an angel twinkling in space
A star is a snowflake in its own place.

A star is treasure golden bright
A star is a jewel with a sparkly light.

A star is an eye spying on God's house
A star is a soft mouse.

A star is a ring on a finger of a king
A star is a feather of a dove's wing.

Catherine Morren (8)
St Mary's Primary School, Greenlough

The Sea

The sea can roar,
The sea can growl,
The sea can bash,
Like a wicked owl.

The sea can be peaceful,
The sea can be free,
The sea can be quiet,
Like a swaying tree.

Tomás Madden (8)
St Mary's Primary School, Greenlough

The Sea

The sea can rip
The sea can tear
The sea can crash
Like an angry bear.

The sea can be slow
The sea can swell
The sea can whisper
Like a tinkling bell.

Aimée Bedell (8)
St Mary's Primary School, Greenlough

The Sea

The sea can rage
The sea can tear
The sea can roar
Like an angry bear.

The sea can be gentle
The sea can be flat
The sea can be friendly
Like a fluffy cat.

Laura McCallion (8)
St Mary's Primary School, Greenlough

Star Shapes

A star is a snowflake so soft
It is like a flying moth.

A star can be white
Like a bright light.

A star is like an angel shining so bright
That is why that star has a light.

The star looks down to spy
But all it can see is a golden eye.

Aidan McErlean (7)
St Mary's Primary School, Greenlough

The Sea

The sea can dash,
The sea can growl,
The sea can roar,
Like a giant owl.

The sea can be breezy,
The sea can be flat,
The sea can be quiet,
Like a sleeping cat.

Jonathan McAteer (8)
St Mary's Primary School, Greenlough

Star Shapes

A star is a teardrop trickling down moon's face.
A star is a bowing snowdrop in God's garden space.

A star is a golden jewel sparkling on a king's crown.
A star is a bright snowflake falling down.

A star is an angel of love,
Spying down from above.

Brendan Laverty (7)
St Mary's Primary School, Greenlough

Gráinne's Mouth

I like my mouth.
My mouth can scream
And eat ice cream.
My mouth can chat,
It can talk to the cat,
It can groan,
But when I'm hurt it will start to moan.
My mouth can smile,
But it can't drive a mile.
My mouth giggled,
While the rest of me wriggled.
My mouth can crunch
And also munch,
My mouth can laugh,
But it can't walk on a path.
My mouth can chew,
But not write the letter Q.
It can taste,
But it has never raced.
My mouth can lick,
Say hi to my dad's friend Rick.
When I'm tired it will start to yawn,
But while I'm playing chess it will not move a pawn.
My mouth can start a fight,
But most of all it will kiss
My mum and dad goodnight.

Gráinne Maguire (8)
St Mary's Primary School, Greenlough

Witch Goes Shopping

There once was a witch
Who was unbelievably rich
And never ran out of money.
She shopped till she dropped
But still never stopped
And bought several jars of honey.

With a magic bean
She created a scene
By dropping her jars of honey.
She shouted like mad
And frightened a lad
And it wasn't at all funny.

Clare Doherty (9)
St Mary's Primary School, Greenlough

Emma's Mouth

I like my mouth.
My mouth can munch my favourite food
And moan when I am in a bad mood.
It can cackle a cheeky laugh,
A roar when I am in the bath.
My mouth can whistle a wonderful tune
And chat to the shining moon.
It can whisper like the tinkling rain
And can squeal out loud when I'm in pain.

Emma McErlain (8)
St Mary's Primary School, Greenlough

Mansion

When I live in a mansion,
I shall keep in my mansion,
Two tiny turtles,
Three tidy tigers,
Four funky pharaohs,
Five famous frogs,
Six slimy slugs,
Seven scared snakes,
Eight embarrassed elephants,
Nine naughty nannies,
Ten toy tractors,
Eleven crawling cows,
Twelve terrible teams and
One ordinary octopus.
That's what I'll have
When I live in my mansion.

Catherine Hegarty (9)
St Mary's Primary School, Greenlough

Happiness Is . . .

Happiness is a roaring drum
It makes me want to run and run.

Happiness is blue and red
The same colours that are on my bed.

Happiness is a cold, rushing stream
Watching it in my dream.

Happiness is a trip to the sea
Come and build sandcastles with me.

Happiness is my family
The way we like to be.

James Duffin (9)
St Mary's Primary School, Greenlough

Liam's Hands

I like my hands.
They can snap
And clap,
Save a goal,
But it always hits the pole,
They can shuffle cards
And win awards,
They can climb a wall
And also break a fall,
They can feel smooth from rough
And punch so tough,
They can help me pick up a book,
But they cannot look.

Liam Quinn (9)
St Mary's Primary School, Greenlough

Happiness Is . . .

Happiness is playing a guitar,
Oh, I love hearing it from afar.

Happiness is brown and white,
It's a chocolate delight.

Happiness is climbing trees
And listening to that soft summer breeze.

Happiness is going to Spain,
Hurry before we miss the plane!

Happiness is my family,
The way they all like to be.

Piaras McGarry (8)
St Mary's Primary School, Greenlough

Roisin's Eyes

My eyes
Can cry,
But also spy,
Stare at my mum,
Glare at my dad,
They can wink
And also blink,
They can open and close like a swinging door,
They can peep at my brother
And gaze at my mother,
My eyes can twinkle when it is bright,
My eyes can dance with pure delight,
My eyes can be green, blue or grey,
They flutter when it's my birthday in May.

Roisin McCloskey (8)
St Mary's Primary School, Greenlough

Worst Spells On Earth

There once was a witch
Who played football on a pitch
She never scored a goal
She had no skills
So the score was always nil-nil.
Oh, why does she hit the pole?

She practised her charms
On big, big farms
And she caused a lot of trouble.
Chickens turned to cows
And geese turned to sows
And her cauldron went hubble bubble.

Robert Kelly (9)
St Mary's Primary School, Greenlough

Colleen's Mouth

I like my mouth.
My mouth mutters and moans,
If I don't get my ice cream cones.
My mouth is as wide as a ship,
It always loves to taste an odd chip.
It argues with my mum,
Sings and even hums.
My mouth can whisper like a church mouse,
And it can roar and shout like an elephant.
My mouth fibs when it chats
And smiles at silly cats.
My mouth laughs loudly at jokes,
That are told to the old folks.
It can talk to an odd goat
And ask how much is a furry coat.
My mouth may munch your mints
And even talk about ancient flints.
It licks lemon lollies
And talks about new hobbies.
My mouth is as round as a ring,
My mouth can do nearly anything.

Colleen McErlean (9)
St Mary's Primary School, Greenlough

Christopher's Eyes

My eyes guide my mummy's trolley,
They help me choose the most delicious lolly,
They cry because I've got a blister
And help spy on my little sister.
My eyes twinkle when I have wonderful stuff,
They are bright with delight when I snatch the last chocolate
And they open wide when I'm surprised.
They can scan my sheets on the internet
And show me when the jelly is set.

Christopher McPeake (8)
St Mary's Primary School, Greenlough

Young Writers - Once Upon A Rhyme Ballymena

My Mansion

When I live in my mansion
I shall keep in my mansion
Two tiny treasures
Three tumbling tricks
Four frightening frogs
Five fair falls
Six smart slugs
Seven super spells
Eight eating elephants
Nine night nurses
Ten talking teddies
Eleven excellent eels
Twelve terrific teachers and
One wonderful waiter.
That's what I'll have
When I live in my mansion.

Olivia Hamill (9)
St Mary's Primary School, Greenlough

Canoeing Is Fun

Sailing by canoe is not a pain,
Relaxed as my hand skims the cool water,
Sailing slowly through the rain,
Paddling to the end of our ride.

Sailing by canoe can be ace,
Delighted as we sail along,
Water splashes my freezing face,
Finally we reach dry land.

Geraldine Scullin (10)
St Mary's Primary School, Greenlough

Sailing Can Be Fun

Sailing on a yacht can be fun,
Happy as the engines run,
Floating past the big bridge,
Bobbing home the sun sets.

Sailing on a yacht can be fun,
Excited as the sail is rising,
Drifting along the massive marina,
Docking at the Pacific port.

Michael Kearney (10)
St Mary's Primary School, Greenlough

Flying In A Space Shuttle

Flying in a space shuttle can be fun,
Excited we'll be there soon,
Staring at silvery stars,
Floating like a balloon.

Flying in a space shuttle can be fun,
Scared as we fly past the sun,
Gasping at the galaxies,
Landing at home.

Declan Laverty (10)
St Mary's Primary School, Greenlough

Star Shapes

A star is a sparkling teardrop in night's face.
A star is a milky snowflake falling from space.

A star is a peaceful angel soaring in God's house.
A star is a quiet snowdrop brightening up the universe.

A star is a winking eye,
So high up in the sky.

Michael McCann (8)
St Mary's Primary School, Greenlough

Riding On A Train

Riding on a train can be fun,
Feeling excited as I talk to my best mate,
Feels like a roller coaster,
I can see the station and I say, 'Great!'

Riding on a train can be fun,
Feeling marvellous as we go,
Scared as we go through the black tunnel,
Don't want to get off, said, 'No!'

Sarah-Louise McPeake (9)
St Mary's Primary School, Greenlough

Riding Can Be Fun

Riding on a quad can be fun,
Feeling frightened going over a bump,
Racing through a smelly dump,
Crashing into the fence.

Riding on a quad can be fun,
Thrilled to get back on,
Racing round my rough lawn,
Making a mess when I'm done.

Stephen Cassidy (10)
St Mary's Primary School, Greenlough

Riding A Bike

Riding a bike can be fun,
Excited to be on my new one,
Zooming down a high hill,
Pedalling for the park.

Riding a bike can be fab,
Worried I'll get a scab,
Skidding on the slippery stones,
Cycling to the circus.

Michael McCloskey (10)
St Mary's Primary School, Greenlough

Riding On A Motorbike

Riding on a motorbike can be fun,
Enjoying the breeze on my face,
Speeding around dangerous corners,
Hoping I'll win the race.

Riding on a motorbike is fun,
Feeling scared that I might crash,
Zooming along the bumpy road,
I'll be home in a flash.

Connor McAllister (10)
St Mary's Primary School, Greenlough

Riding On A Go-Kart Can Be Fun

Riding on a go-kart can be fun,
Happy to do it twice,
Racing my mate in the sun,
When I am eight years old.

Riding on a go-kart can be fun,
Pleased to get a go,
Happy I got a turn,
Braking, I go off the track.

Cathal McGurk (10)
St Mary's Primary School, Greenlough

Riding On A Horse

Riding a horse can be fun,
Excited as I sit in the saddle,
Leaping and landing over the jumps,
Patting my horse in the sun.

Riding a horse is just great,
Enthusiastic as I kick to start,
Pacing around the paddock,
Dismount and close the gate.

Brid Mackle (10)
St Mary's Primary School, Greenlough

Young Writers - Once Upon A Rhyme Ballymena

Snowboards Can Be Great

Travelling by snowboard can be fun,
Scared as I skid through a forest,
Dodging sharp stones until there is none,
Boarding through a twisty tunnel.

Travelling by snowboard can be great,
Shocked as I slide over icy ground,
Leaping little rivers, going into a straight,
Finally at the finish.

Michael Scullin (10)
St Mary's Primary School, Greenlough

Ice Skates Can Be Fun

Travelling on ice skates can be fun,
Eager to get on the ice,
I am nearly as fast as a sledge,
Gliding along to the edge.

Travelling on ice skates can be fun,
Happy to be on the ice,
I fall,
I hear silence in the hall.

Matthew Henry (9)
St Mary's Primary School, Greenlough

Sailing On A Raft Can Be Fun

Sailing on a raft can be fun,
Happy to get on without sinking,
Almost tipping to the side,
Lots of fun I'm having.

Sailing on a raft can be fun,
Glad I'm sailing it,
Kneeling is sore on my knees,
Oh no, we've taken a hit.

Enda McNally (10)
St Mary's Primary School, Greenlough

Travelling By Plane

Flying by plane can be fun,
Nervous as I go up the steps,
Gazing at the calm countryside,
The plane starts to glide.

Flying on a plane can be fun,
Scared that the plane will crash,
Flying past lovely pieces of land,
The plane taxies to its stand.

Fionnuala Scullin (9)
St Mary's Primary School, Greenlough

My Friend Always Cares For Me

My friend always cares for me
Even when I'm bad.
My friend always cares for me
When I'm very sad.
My friend always cares for me
In every little way
And I think she is the very best
What else can I say?

My friend always cares for me
Even when I boss.
My friend always cares for me
Even when I'm cross.
My friend always cares for me
In every little way
And I think she is the very best
What else can I say?

Joanne Rodgers (9)
The Diamond Primary School

We're Off To The Shops

We're off to the shops
And there's lots to buy.
We can buy . . .

Red apples
Yellow bananas
Green grapes
Black berries
Orange oranges
White flour
Red roses
Purple berries
Yellow corn
Red grapes
Yellow lemons
Green pears
White sugar
Brown sauce.

Gareth Workman (10)
The Diamond Primary School

We're Off To The Shops

We're off to the shops
And there's lots to buy.
We can buy . . .
Red apples
Yellow bananas
Green cabbages
Brown doughnuts
White eggs
Silver fish
Red grapes
Pink ham
Chocolate ice cream!

Beverley Kerr (11)
The Diamond Primary School

We're Off To The Shops

We're off to the shops
And there's lots to buy.
We can buy:
Apricots and
Apples and
Bananas and
Beetroot and
Cherries and
Celery and
Doughnuts and
Dates and
Eggs and
Egg noodles and
French fries and
Fish and
Grapefruit and
Grapes and
Ham and
Honey and
Icing and
Irish stew.

Nicola Simpson (10)
The Diamond Primary School

My Daddy

D is for my daddy,
A is for all the things he does for me,
D is for drawing plans for houses,
D is for driving a big jeep,
Y is for Yorkie bars. Daddy loves them.

Matthew Kirk (7)
The Diamond Primary School

My Best Friend

My best friend is loving and always cares for me
If I'm sad and down
He always cheers me up
If I forget my pencils
He always shares with me.

My best friend is funny and always makes me laugh
When he's at my house, I can't stop laughing at the things he does
Like jumping into dirty puddles
And jumping out of trees
I hope we stay like this
Until life ends.

Reuben Bailie (8)
The Diamond Primary School

We're Off To The Shops

We're off to the shops
And there's lots to buy.
We can buy . . .

Apples and
Bananas and
Chips and
Doughnuts and
Eggs and
Fish and
Grapes and
Ham and
Ice cream.

Amy Greer (11)
The Diamond Primary School

One Cold Winter's Night

Outside on the frosty streets
In the winter's night
Snow falls gently
Not a sound
Silence all around.
All the people stuck indoors
Sleeping in their beds
Gently dreaming, floorboards creaking
Santa's coming to town.

'Ho, ho, ho,' he gently says
Leaving presents
Under the tree
When the children all wake up
Smiles are coming joyfully.

Excitement flows through children and adults
You as much as me
Everyone gives
Children play
Until it's time
To receive.

Lee Millar (9)
The Diamond Primary School

Gerbil

G is for my messy gerbil,
E is for the eating he does,
R is for really good things he does,
B is for the nasty bite he gave Mandy,
 I is for into the house where he loves to sleep,
L is for the lovely water he drinks.

Trevor Holmes (8)
The Diamond Primary School

Hello/Goodbye

Hello holidays
Goodbye home

Hello homework
Goodbye school

Hello school
Goodbye bed

Hello Mummy
Goodbye Daddy

Hello poetry
Goodbye math

Hello dinner
Goodbye lunch

Hello TV
Goodbye homework

Hello Wednesday
Goodbye Tuesday

Hello Janelle and Melissa
Goodbye Adam and Matthew

Hello morning
Goodbye night

Hello children
Goodbye grown-ups!

Hannah Kirk (8)
The Diamond Primary School

My Piano

P is for piano. I like to play the notes of 'The Big Bad Boat'
I is for ink on my piano book
A is for my auntie - she plays the piano in assembly
N is for naughty little notes that I can play
O is for Little Oscar Otter who shows me the notes on my piano.

Kirsty Speers (7)
The Diamond Primary School

My Dog Dixon

M unching and crunching his food to bits
Y elping and barking all night in his bed.

D ancing and wagging his tail
O ranges that he loves to bite
G rabbing and eating secret treats.

D og biscuits being eaten by him
I brush him every day
X mas leftovers that I gave him
O n Sundays we take him for a short walk
N othing but sleeping all day!

Jonathan Jordan (9)
The Diamond Primary School

Colour Poem

Red is a roaring motorbike,
Gold is the lovely golden sun,
Blue is a big New Holland,
Green is the lovely grass,
White is all the fluffy clouds,
Orange is the enormous bonfire,
Black is a nice, cute cow,
Brown is the trunk of a giant pine tree.

Gareth Harkness (9)
The Diamond Primary School

A Wonderful Friend

When I fall, my friend help
She never says cry baby.
When I go to play with her
She doesn't say you're not playing.
When it's her birthday
She always invites me.
When I talk
She always listens.
When I forget my pencil case
She says, 'You can borrow mine.'
When I'm sick
She comes to my house and entertains me.
When I forget my packed lunch
She shares hers.
When I ask her to a sleepover
She says, 'Why not?'
When I'm stuck in English or math
She helps me out.
When it's my birthday
She's the one who buys me the biggest present.
When we go up town together
She buys me a bracelet.
When I tell her a joke
She laughs, she doesn't say, 'That's silly.'
When I need her
She's always there for me.

Janelle McCloy (9)
The Diamond Primary School

My Cat, Tiddles

M iaowing all the time
Y elling at the door for food.

C at food to buy for him
A ttacking mice and chasing rabbits
T ingling and bouncing, his bell rings loudly.

T enderly running my hands through his fur
I stroke my cat when he is good
D angerously walking on wood
D eadly things that he does
L oving the food we give him
E verything we give him is gone so quickly
S heltered at night-time when he comes in from hunting.

Ryan Smyth (9)
The Diamond Primary School

Farming

F is for farming in the mud
A is for eating lovely apples
R is for revving up the tractor
M is for the cows munching the grass
I is for into the field we go
N is for the cows nodding
G is for opening the gates.

Stewart McDonald (8)
The Diamond Primary School

Colour Poem

Green is like the grass
That grows outside,
The leaves that blow
In the wind,
The fields that are enormous.

Red is like a car
That is shiny,
A door that opens
And closes,
Your face
When you're embarrassed.

Blue is like the sky
That hangs from the air,
The fish
That are in the sea,
Eyes of people like me!

Orange is like a cat
That my friend has,
An orange
That people eat,
The sun that is so hot.

David Simpson (8)
The Diamond Primary School

Farming

F is for farming.
A is for watching animals in the field.
R is for riding on the tractor.
M is for mixing slurry.
I is for in the farmyard we go.
N is for never drive tractors on your own.
G is for opening the gates.

Mark Patterson (7)
The Diamond Primary School

Makes Me Think

Winter makes me think of white snow,
Snow makes me think of the cold ice,
Ice makes me think of the dripping icicles,
Icicles make me think of the cold water,
Water makes me think of lovely hot drinks,
Drinks make me think of the hot fire,
Fire makes me think of winter.

Victoria Henry (9)
The Diamond Primary School

Diesel

There once was a dog called Diesel,
He liked to play with a weasel.
Every day and every night,
He liked to play and bite,
Sometimes he got too close
And banged his head on the post.

Hannah Smyth (7)
The Diamond Primary School